FERDINAND LASSALLE

FERDINAND LASSALLE

AS A SOCIAL REFORMER

BY

(EDWARD BERNSTEIN)

FORMERLY EDITOR OF "DER SOZIAL DEMOCRAT."

TRANSLATED BY ELEANOR MARX AVELING

GREENWOOD PRESS, PUBLISHERS
NEW YORK

Originally published in 1893
by Swan Sonnenschein & Sons, London

First Greenwood Reprinting, 1969

Library of Congress Catalogue Card Number 69-13824

PREFACE.

THE short account of Lassalle here submitted to the English reader is, with some slight alterations, a translation of my Introduction to the complete edition of Lassalle's *Speeches and Works*. I was asked to edit these by the executive of the German Social-Democratic Party of Germany in the spring of 1891. In the German this Introduction bears the title *Ferdinand Lassalle and his Significance in the History of Social-Democracy*. I did not adopt the same title for the English edition in order to avoid confusion between my own and other works already published in England under similar titles. Indeed, this sketch is not intended to compete with elaborate works like that of Mr. W. H. Dawson. It is intended rather to act as a complement to Mr. Dawson's book and other works dealing with Lassalle and German Social-Democracy. For a full treatment of the subject it is far too incomplete, and its constituent parts are of purpose unequally balanced. Thus many important statements and criticisms were in the original reserved for the special introductions to the various works of Lassalle, and these I have not incorporated in the English volume. But, on the other hand, it deals with questions almost ignored by other writers, and after I have had access to documents hitherto unknown to them. Further, it is written at the same time from a Social-Democratic and a critical standpoint, whilst other critics of Lassalle have mostly been more or less opposed to Social-Democracy, or, in the case of Socialists who have written about him, they either did not criticise him at all, or criticised only his acts, and did not enter into any analysis of his theories. But such treatment of the subject is indispensable now that Lassalle is being exploited by the enemies of Socialism against Social-Democracy.

It is undeniable that Socialism in Germany to-day has no resemblance to the special characteristics of Ferdinand Lassalle's Socialism. The more this became evident, the more Lassalle became the hero of the middle-class *littérateur*, and was held up as the "good" Socialist, as opposed by the middle-class politician to the "bad" Social-Democrats of to-day. Was he not a *national* patriot, in contrast to the unpatriotic internationalists, destitute of "fatherland" —the followers of Karl Marx and Frederick Engels? Was he not a real statesman, as compared with these mere demagogues or abstract theorists? Had he not, at least, a scheme, even though it may have been wrong, for bringing about the peaceful socialisation of society, whilst these men do nothing but draw bills on a future revolution?

With all this cant we have had to deal in Germany, and that it has been imported into England is only too evident. This is why I have allowed passages dealing with this point to remain unabridged in the translation.

The reader will at once see that my standpoint is that of Karl Marx and Fr. Engels, whose doctrines are to-day accepted by the Socialist Parties—with some few exceptions— all over the world. Many misrepresentations and misunderstandings have been circulated as to the relation of Ferdinand Lassalle's Socialism to these doctrines, and as to his personal relations with the author of *Das Kapital*. To some Lassalle is a disciple of Marx and Engels, who only differed from them on the question of productive co-operative associations; to others he is an original Socialist thinker, who merely took a few details of his criticism of capitalist production from Marx. Neither view holds good on closer examination. Lassalle was much more in-debted to Marx than he admitted in his writings ; but he was a disciple of Marx only in a restricted sense. As to the former point, even in the book in which he speaks of Marx—*Herr Bastiat-Schulze*—Lassalle takes much more than he acknowledges from the book of Marx to which he refers. Very important deductions and even quotations from this book are made use of without any allusion to the original. In his speeches and pamphlets, again, in which he never refers to any of his Socialist predecessors, the in-fluence of these must strike the reader acquainted with Socialist literature. This does not apply to Marx and Engels only, but also to Louis Blanc and other French Socialists.

The points in which Lassalle—sometimes consciously, sometimes unconsciously—differed from Marx and Engels I have dealt with explicitly in this book, and therefore I need not recapitulate them here. But upon one point a few words should be said, as it bears upon a question much discussed recently on this side of the channel.

Marx has been reproached—and this even by a section of English Socialists—with basing his Socialism upon the Ricardian theory of value adopted, and but slightly modi-fied by him. In his *History of Socialism*, written, on the whole, in the fairest spirit, Mr. Thomas Kirkup, *e.g.*, says that when the Economists did not follow the Ricardian principle to its obvious conclusion—" that if labour is the source of wealth, the labourer should enjoy it all," it was " otherwise with the Socialists," and " as posited by the Economists, and applied by the Socialists, Marx accepted the principle." It "was made and continues to be, the foundation-stone of the system of Marx, and is really its weakest point." (Page 147.)

Now, already in the treatise which Mr. Kirkup quotes on this occasion, the *Misère de la Philosophie*, written and published in 1847, Marx says—"All the egalitarian conclusions which Mr. Proudhon draws from Ricardo's theory are based upon a fundamental error, for he confuses the value of commodities measured by the *quantity of labour* embodied in them with the value of commodities incurred by *the value of labour*" (p. 31 of the French, and p. 30 of the first German editions). After showing why and how this is inadmissible, Marx gives the names of the English Socialists who before Proudhon—who posed as the inventor of the idea—had made an "egalitarian" application of Ricardo's formula, and gives as examples passages from Bray's *Labour's Wrongs and Labour's Remedies*, London, 1839. And afterwards he proves that Bray's ideal of improving society by following out Ricardo's theory "to its obvious conclusion" is nothing but the reflex of society as it is.

This was written, as I have said, in 1847, *i.e.*, at a time when Marx had not yet completely worked out his own theory. Even then he saw clearly that what Mr. Kirkup, in accordance with, or may I say, misled by, many other writers, calls " the foundation-stone of the system of Marx " was a theoretical impossibility. In his *Zur Kritik der Politischen Œkonomie*, published in 1859, Marx refers again to the egalitarian application of Ricardo's formula by English Socialists, and again makes it clear that he does not agree with them. He states four objections to the Ricardian theory of value (the second of which is the one taken up by these Socialists), and lays them down as so many problems to be solved by a closer analysis of the society from which the Ricardian theory is drawn, *viz.*, modern capitalist society. A little further on he quotes John Gray, another

English Socialist, earlier in date than Bray, who attempted an egalitarian application of Ricardo's formula, and again proves its fallacies and intrinsic contradictions (c. i., p. 40, and pp. 61-64).[1]

In *Das Kapital* Mr. Kirkup could have read, firstly, that "labour is *not* the only source of material wealth" (p. 18 of the second edition of the German edition, and p. 10 of the English). Wealth and exchange value are two very different things. Secondly, although Marx lays bare all the tricks of capitalist exploitation of the workers, he does not by a single word claim for the workers "the full value of their labour." Why not? Because, as he shows, "value," in an economic sense, is a quality belonging to commodities only, and which, therefore, can only occur in a society where products are exchanged as commodities, the value of a commodity being measured by the socially necessary labour embodied in it. Labour being, therefore, the measure of value, can have no value of its own. But it is quite different with the labour-power of the workers. This labour-power in our actual state of society is a commodity, is recognised as such by all political economists, and, therefore, not only can have, but actually has, a value. And this value is determined by the quantity of socially necessary labour required for its production, maintenance,

---

[1] Here, too, as in *La Misère de la Philosophie*, Marx refers to W. Thompson's *Inquiry into the Distribution of Wealth, &c.*, as a book which went wrong on the same question. This alone should have warned readers against accepting the assertion of Dr. A. Menger, repeated by English critics, that Marx took his theory of surplus value from Thompson, an assertion based upon nothing but the fact that the *words* surplus value are occasionally used by Thompson; but anyone who takes the trouble to read Thompson's book will at once find that surplus value with him is quite another thing than surplus value as defined by Marx. Cf. the article *Juristen Sozialismus* in the *Neue Zeit*, year 1887, pp. 49 *sqq.*

and reproduction, that is to say, required for the production, maintenance, and reproduction of the actually living
labourer. The price of this labour-power or the rate of
wages may at a given time be higher, and at another lower
than the actual value of labour-power, as the same thing
occurs with the prices of commodities ; but whatever form
the wages take, whether that of time-wages or piece-wages,
under our system of capitalist production, based upon competition, they are but the price of labour-power. Now, if
in the assertion that the workers are entitled to the full
value of their labour, by labour is meant labour-power,
that would mean no change in the present conditions ; but
if it is to mean the full value of the product of their labour,
that would mean the abolition of capitalistic production,
and, with it, of the category of "value" altogether.

To put it in the words of Frederick Engels : "The conclusion drawn from the Ricardian theory, that to the
workers, the only real producers, belongs the sum total of
the product of society, *their* product, this conclusion leads
directly into communism. But from a purely economical
point of view, it is no argument at all, for it is but an application of moral rules to political economy. According
to the laws of political economy, the larger share of the
product does *not* go to the workers who have produced it.
If, now, we say : this is wrong, this ought not to be, we
assert something which *prima facie* does not concern political economy at all. We merely state that this economical
fact is in contradiction with our moral sentiments. *Marx,
therefore, never based his communistic demands upon this
argument, but upon the inevitable breakdown of capitalist
production, a breakdown the evidences of which are becoming
more palpably apparent every day.* He only says that surplus value consists of unpaid labour, which is simply stating

a fact. But a statement may be economically wrong in form, and yet right historically. If the moral conscience of the masses declares an economical fact to be unjust, as it did in former epochs declare slavery or corvée labour to be unjust, this is a proof that this same fact has outlived itself, that other economical facts have come into being, in consequence of which the former has become unbearable and untenable. Such an application of economical theory, though formally wrong, may therefore hide an economical truth of undoubted reality." (Preface to the German translation of *La Philosophie de la Misère*, first edition, pp. 10, 11.)

And Marx sums up the result of his researches in the first volume of *Das Kapital* by saying that the impending expropriation of the expropriators will establish individual property, based on the acquisition of the capitalist era, *i.e.*, on co-operation and possession in common of the land and of the means of production. There is nothing said here of the mode of distribution of wealth corresponding to that new state of society. But this reconstructed society will not come into being all at once, ready-made like Minerva ; it will be subject to evolution as well as society in the past, and therefore the mode of the distribution of wealth will vary with the different phases of its evolution. It will depend upon the degree in which the economical, intellectual, and moral emancipation from capitalism shall have been accomplished. It will depend also upon the mass of wealth at the command of society, and upon many other questions. In a letter written in 1875, criticising the programme of the newly united Socialist party in Germany, and published in *Die Neue Zeit* (vol. i., p. 565, 1890-1891), Marx has fully explained his views on this point.

But if Marx did not base his Socialism on the Ricardian

theory of value, this cannot be asserted of Lassalle. He took his economic criticism of capitalist society from the then published works of Marx and Engels, but for his remedy he had recourse to the French and earlier English Socialists. To counteract the Ricardian law of wages, which he accepted in full, even along with its Malthusian foundation, he proposed as a remedy co-operative productive associations, subventioned by the State. I have shown in Chapter VII. of this book why, in my opinion, his remedy was wrong.

A few words upon another question—the question of political tactics. In reading over this book again, it strikes me that in some respects the situation it describes resembles the situation in England at the present time. In England also we see a young Socialist party striving to secure a position independent of the existing political parties. Thus the criticisms upon the tactics of Lassalle might also be taken as applying to the tactics of my English comrades. I therefore ask the reader to keep in mind that in Prussia at the time of Lassalle there existed only a sham constitutionalism. Parliament did not rule, but the King and his Ministers, Parliament possessing only a very restricted veto. All the powers of government were in the hands of the Crown and the classes behind it : the aristocracy, the small but influential party of landlords and Church bigots, the military, and bureaucracy. In Prussia, least of all, therefore, was it good policy to let oneself be seduced by the cry of " no political but economic reforms." It meant, as this mostly means, neither the one nor the other. The battle-cry of the workers, as long as they have not secured the political rights necessary to make them the rulers of society, must always be: "political *and* economic reforms."

When in 1866 the North German Confederation was

founded, manhood suffrage was granted for the Reichstag, while certain restrictive laws affecting working-men's trade societies and strikes were abolished. The foundation of the German Empire in 1871 wrought no change in this respect. In Prussia and other German States the "three class" electoral system (see page 7), or rather high census franchises, still exists, and neither the Reichstag nor the State diets have the power to enforce Bills of their own. A Bill agreed to by five-sixths of the Reichstag is useless, or worse than useless, if the Federal Government will not consider it. And there is no likelihood that this degrading state will be altered by our German middle-classes, or that any serious steps in this direction will be taken by them.

But if little progress has been made with regard to political rights in Germany since the days of Lassalle, economical and social progress has proceeded by leaps and bounds. A few facts to illustrate this.

In 1860, the value of yearly manufacture was in millions of pounds sterling, 310 in Germany, 380 in France, 577 in the United Kingdom. In 1888 it was 583 in Germany, 485 in France, 820 in the United Kingdom. The steam-power used was (expressed in thousands of horse-power):—

	United Kingdom.	France.	Germany.
1860	2450	1120	850
1870	4040	1850	2480
1888	9200	4520	6200

And if we take only the steam-power of fixed engines, *i.e.*, that used for *manufacturing purposes*, we have this result:—

	United Kingdom.	France.	Germany.
1860	700,000	181,000	200,000
1870	940,000	341,000	900,000
1888	2,200,000	695,500[1]	2,000,000

(Mulhall's *Dictionary of Statistics*, 1892, pp. 365, 545, etc.)

[1] These figures (for France) apply to the year 1885.

If the German middle-class have not fulfilled their political mission as the British and the French middle-classes
did in their time, they are the more eager to fulfil their
economic mission.   The frequent statement that the wonderful growth of Social-Democracy in Germany is only the
result of the backward condition of economical and political conditions in Germany is based on very little knowledge of actual facts.   It is true that the defective political
institutions of the empire account, to a certain extent, for
the growth of the " subversive " party ; but that growth is
still more accounted for by the economical development—
one might almost say the economic revolution—of the last
twenty or thirty years.   Industrially, Germany is already too
advanced for our middle-classes to be inclined to seriously
fight the Monarchy.   Having regard to the immense numbers of the proletariat in the many rapidly growing towns,
they think it better to do as monarchs do elsewhere—to
reign, but not to govern.   There have been, and there will
be, between semi-absolutist monarchs and the German
bourgeoisie, only little family disagreements, which have
been, and may again be noisy wrangles, but will never lead
to any serious struggle.   Both know too well that they
have need of each other.   Social-Democracy, besides its
own historical mission, has to complete the unfulfilled
missions of its predecessors.

In a few passages I refer to England.   In respect to
them, the reader will kindly remember that they were
originally addressed to, and intended for, a German public.

EDWARD BERNSTEIN.

CONTENTS.

FERDINAND LASSALLE.

CHAPTER I.

So long as there have been ruling and oppressed, exploiting and
exploited classes, there have also been revolts of the latter against
the former; there have been statesmen and philosophers, self-
seekers and enthusiasts, who have proposed certain social reforms
for the mending or for the ending of these conditions of exploitation. If all these efforts are to be summed up under the head
of Socialism, then Socialism is as old as civilisation. But if we
keep to more definite characteristics than the mere desire for a
harmonious state of society and universal well-being, the Socialism
of to-day has only this much in common with that of any former
epoch, that it, like these, is the reflex of the special conditions of
the class-struggle of its time. In all cases the structure of the
society upon whose soil it has grown, sets its stamp upon the
Socialism of the particular epoch.

Modern Socialism is the product of the class-war in capitalist
Society; it has its root in the class-antagonism between the bourgeoisie and the modern proletariat, an antagonism that finds
expression, in actual struggle, comparatively early in history, although, it is true, the combatants themselves did not at first grasp
its exact bearing. In its revolt against the privileged classes of
Feudal Society, as in its struggle against State absolutism, the
middle-class is induced to assume the part of advocate of the interests of all the non-privileged, and it is always in the name of

the whole people that it demands the abolition of institutions unfavourable, and the creation of institutions necessary, to the development of its own forces.   And in this the middle-class acts, for
a long time, in good faith, since only the ideas which it itself con-
nects with these demands appear to it rational and commendable
to the sound common-sense of humanity.   The rising proletariat,
however, so far as it has freed itself from the prejudices of the
guild burghers, takes the promises of the middle-class spokesmen
for sterling coin, so long as that middle-class is exclusively in
opposition to the representatives of existing institutions.   But
once it has conquered the latter, or has, at least, so far beaten
them, that it can set about realizing its own aspirations, it becomes evident that the plebeians behind it have an altogether
different conception of the promised Kingdom of Heaven upon
earth from that of their quondam friends and protectors, and
the result is strife, the more violent the greater have been the
former illusions.   But the proletariat is not yet powerful enough
to keep up its resistance; it is forced into silence by ruthless
violence, and disappears again, for a long time, from the scene of
action.

This was the case in all the middle-class risings of the sixteenth, seventeenth, and eighteenth, and even in the first decades of the nineteenth century.   The rapid development in the
revolution of the conditions of production, during the century,
have, however, changed the relation of the proletariat *vis-à-vis* of
the bourgeoisie.   Exceptional circumstances were no longer
needed to make manifest the antagonism between the interests
and aims of these two, and without these that antagonism found
expression in the more advanced countries.   Workers began to
organise for resistance against the capitalist class; bourgeois
conditions of society were subjected to criticism from the proletarian standpoint; an anti-bourgeois, Socialist literature arose.
Relatively unimportant dissensions within the bosom of the bourgeoisie itself, the simple conflict of one of its wings with
another, sufficed to allow the more active elements of the proletariat to enter the lists as an independent party, with demands

of its own. The Reform movement of middle-class liberalism in
England was the signal for the Chartist movement; the July
Revolution in France inaugurated first a purely Republican, but
then a Socialist and revolutionary proletarian propaganda, which,
in importance, scarcely fell short of the Chartist agitation.

In the forties the movement—literary and propagandist—
passes to Germany. Writers and politicians, who had been
abroad, either as exiles, or in order, for a while at least, to escape
the smell of the police at home—become proselytes of Socialism,
and seek to transplant it to Germany. German artizans, who,
during their "Wanderschaft,"[1] had worked in Paris or London,
bring the Socialist teaching picked up there back to their homes,
and carry it from one house of call to the next. Secret revolutionary propagandist societies are started, and finally, on the eve
of the year of Revolution, 1848, the Communist League comes
into existence with a programme that proclaims with unsurpas-
sable revolutionary keenness and clearness the antagonism between proletariat and bourgeoisie. But it also declares that the
peculiar conditions in Germany made it necessary for the proletariat to fight, for the time being, alongside of the bourgeoisie
against absolute monarchy, feudal squirearchy, and petty bourgeoisie.[2]

The February Revolution in France, and the March Revolution
in Germany, found the former, in its chief centres, absolutely
honeycombed with Socialism, and found the latter permeated by a
relatively large number of socialistic, and socialistically-inclined
workers. In Germany, as in France, the workers already supplied, though possibly not in the same proportion, the most active

[1] The mediæval custom of journeymen travelling from place to place,
and even country to country, was, and to some extent still is, kept up in
Germany. The "*Herbergen*," or houses of call, are the inns and hostelries
where, on their journeys, they put up.

[2] "In Germany, they, [the Communists] fight with the bourgeoisie
whenever it acts in a revolutionary way against the absolute monarchy,
the feudal squirearchy, and the petty bourgeoisie." ["Manifesto of the
Communist Party," by Karl Marx and Frederick Engels. Translated from
the German by S. Moore (published in 1847), and published by W. Reeves.]

elements of the Revolution. But the conditions in France, despite her political and economic superiority, were not much more propitious for the realising of Socialism than were those of Germany. In the country small peasant proprietorship predominated, while in the town and industrial centres, although the Grand Industry had made great strides, it had not conquered a complete monopoly. By the side of it there existed—and this chiefly in Paris, the main centre of the trade in *articles de luxe*—handicraft on a smaller and larger scale, which, if it had lost its old guild-like character, and was worked mostly for large employers, still played a relatively important part, more especially in the so-called "artistic" handicrafts. Consequently, French Socialism, even where it had freed itself from mere Utopianism, was only of the petty bourgeois type. Nor did even the February Revolution, and the terrible lesson of the June massacre make any difference. They gave the death-blow to Utopian Socialism among the French workers, but in its stead there appeared for many a year—Proudhonism.

In this relative unripeness of the economic conditions lies the explanation of the otherwise incomprehensible fact, that while the France of this period swarmed with Socialists, while over two hundred members of the Chamber of Deputies called themselves " Social Democrats," the Bonapartist tyranny was able to put the workers off with empty phrases.

In Germany the unripeness was, of course, even greater. The great mass of the workers was not merely imbued with the petty bourgeois spirit, but to some extent actually with that of the mediæval guilds. At the various working-men's congresses which 1848 called into existence, the most reactionary propositions were discussed. Only a comparatively small minority of the German workers had grasped the revolutionary mission of the working-class. If they everywhere fought in the front rank of the advanced parties; if, wherever they could, they tried to urge on the middle-class democracy, they paid the cost of all this in their own person. The Communists of 1848 fell on the barricades, on the battle-field of Baden ; they filled the prisons, or they were obliged, when the reaction triumphed all along the line, to go into exile, where a large number of them died in misery. The young working-men's organisations, which the spring of 1848 had called into existence, were indiscriminately dissolved by the Government, or worried literally to death.

Such Socialists as still remained in the country either entirely withdrew from public life, in the hope of better times, or became Philistine, and joined whatever seemed to them the most likely faction of bourgeois liberalism. This applies more especially to the spokesmen of the " semi-cultured," " semi-sans-culotte," "true" Socialism, who had made their appearance with such great *éclat*. But the workers themselves, more or less intimidated, gave up all thought of their organisation as a class with independent aims, and fell under the tutelage of the radical bourgeois parties, or the protection of well-meaning bourgeois philanthropists. A development came about which, in all essentials, agreed with that which had preceded it in England and France under similar conditions. The failure of the renewed agitation of the Chartists, in the year 1848, had the effect in England of forcing to the front the Christian Socialism of the Maurices, Kingsleys, Ludlows, and induced a portion of the workers to seek their emancipation in self-help co-operative associations—not only their economic but their "moral" emancipation from "egotism," "class-hatred," etc. And if these Christian Socialists did not combine with their efforts selfish, personal aims, and if they did not help to grind the axes of any one of the parties of the possessing classes, the result of their propaganda among the workers— so far as its influence went—was none the less to divert them from the general interest of their class, *i.e.*, was one of political emasculation. So far as they succeeded in getting rid of "class-egotism," this was, in most cases, replaced by a disgusting egotism of co-operation, and a not less disgusting cant of "culture." The Trades Union movement, on its side, was almost wholly absorbed in the pursuit of only its most immediate interests, while most of the Owenites threw in their lot with the so-called Free-thought movement.

In France it was the defeat of the June Insurrection that forced the working-class into the background of the revolutionary arena. At first, however, only into the background. Not even that colossal blood-letting had been able to kill the strong political spirit of the Parisian proletariat, which, as Marx says in the "Achtzehnter Brumaire," always tries to press forward again whenever the movement appears to make a fresh start.

Nevertheless, its strength was broken; it could no longer obtain even a momentary triumph. " As soon as one of the upper strata of Society is stirred by a revolutionary ferment, the proletariat enters into a union with it, and so shares all the defeats which the different parties experience one after another. But these retro-active blows grow weaker and weaker, the more they are spread over the whole surface of Society. Its more notable leaders in public assemblies and in the press, one after the other, fall victims to the Law, and figures more and more equivocal appear at its head. In fact, it throws itself into doctrinaire experiments, ex-change banks and workers' associations, into a movement, there-fore, in which it gives up revolutionising the old world with its great collective means, but rather seeks, behind the back of Society, by individual effort, within its own narrow conditions of existence, to bring about its redemption, and, therefore, of necessity fails." (18 Brumaire, 3rd ed., pp. 14 and 15.)

Finally, in Germany also, where there can be no question of an actual defeat of the workers, since they had not yet even sought to take any considerable action as a class, all attempts worth speaking of, on the part of the workers at independent action, remained for a long time in abeyance. While middle-class philanthropy was busying itself in clubs " for the benefit of the working-classes," with questions of the housing of the working-classes, sick funds, and other harmless matters, a democrat of the petty bourgeois class, the Prussian Member of Parliament, Schulze of Delitzsch, started solving the social question by founding self-help co-operative societies, in which praiseworthy undertaking the economic backwardness of Germany stood him in especially good stead.

From the very outset, Herr Schulze-Delitzsch had intended his co-operative societies not only for the workers, but also for the small handicraft masters ; these were, by means of credit and raw material clubs, to be enabled to compete with modern industry. And as modern industry was but little developed in Germany, and as, on the other hand, there were large numbers of small masters, who had not yet, like the small masters in France and in England, adapted themselves to the conditions of modern industry, but were rather on the look-out for some sort of protection against it, his idea was bound, so far as they were concerned, to fall on fruitful soil, since these co-operative associations, in so far as modern industry had not appropriated their particular branches of production, really were of some use to them. So the credit and raw material associations blossomed forth gaily, and together with them distributive associations also, while in the background—as crown of the whole—loomed the productive co-operative associations that were to be the realisation of the freeing of labour from capital. Just as little as the English Christian Socialists, did Herr Schulze-Delitzsch wish to further the interests of any political party by his self-help co-operative propaganda ; like them he was simply practising a philanthropy in harmony with his class instincts. At the time when he started this movement, the party to which he belonged—the left of the Prussian National Assembly—had withdrawn from active political life. After this party had let the Government and its beloved squirearchy lead it by the nose after the most approved fashion, it had, when the Prussian Government insisted upon introducing the "three-class" [1] electoral system,

---

[1] The "three-class" electoral system is roughly this : the whole of the taxes in any given parish, ward, or district, forming a unit of any electoral constituency, are lumped together, and the sum thus obtained is divided into three parts. Those persons paying the highest taxes, *i.e.*, one-third of the whole amount, form the "first class" voters ; those paying the second-third, the "second class," and the rest of the tax-payers form the "third class." Each class elects two "electors" ("Wahlmänner"), and all the "electors" of a constituency elect two members to the diet. The whole of the voting is open. Thus all the voting can be watched by the authorities, employers, etc. Moreover, the votes are restricted to tax-payers, and the

done the wisest thing it could do : it had clenched its fists in its pockets, and left the reaction to settle their own hash.

Petty bourgeois from the crown of his head to the sole of his foot—but petty bourgeois with liberal views, and well-meaning in his way, Schulze-Delitzsch, after he had been prosecuted by the reaction, took up an idea which was then in the air. "Association" had been the cry of the Socialists in the thirties and forties ; "association" now cried the bourgeois philanthropists, ; "association" dogmatised the Conservative writer, B. A. Huber. Why should not the Liberal district Judge Schulze also plead for "association"?

As we shall have to consider the association question later on, we here only quote a few passages from a work of Schulze-Delitzsch, published in 1858, in which he tells us the effect he expects his co-operative associations to have upon the condition of the workers. "And as regards those workers who are still wage workers, the competition of the co-operative associations with the employers has, for them also, the most beneficial results. For must not the increased demand, on the part of the employer, tend to raise the wages of the workers? Are not the proprietors of large works thus obliged to offer their employees the very best conditions of labour, because they otherwise risk their men going over to already existing co-operative associations, or indeed, of themselves starting one, a proceeding to which, of course, the ablest and most energetic workers would most incline? Assuredly, only by these means—*by the workers themselves competing with the employers*—can wages be permanently raised, and the conditions of labour generally improved,

wealthy classes can always outvote the mass of the people. It has happened, for example, that a single individual has represented the whole first class electorate, and has alone nominated two "electors." There are rarely more than a score of "first class" voters ; the "second class" number three or four times as many, the "third class" seventeen or eighteen times as many as the "first class." No wonder Prince Bismarck at one time denounced this system as "the most wretched of all electoral systems." It is true this was at a time when the Prussian middle-class opposed him. He afterwards opposed every effort to do away with, or even to amend, the system.

and never, as we have seen, can this be permanently accomplished by compulsory laws or by appeals to humanity. . . . ."

" When once a number of such co-operative establishments have been started by working-men, and the existing monopoly of the large employers has thus been broken down, it is inevitable that the enormous profits formerly reaped by them alone will diminish, because they will be obliged to let the workers have their share of them. Thus, while wealth on the one hand will assume rather more modest dimensions, poverty will, on the other, disappear more and more, and conditions will begin to tend towards a universal level of well-being. With this also a bound is set both to plutocracy and to pauperism, those unholy outgrowths of our industrial system, in which we see two powers equally hostile to true culture. . . . "

" Only, we must constantly insist upon this : that until the workers of their own strength and impulse venture to start such undertakings, and to practically demonstrate that they can carry them on alone without the participation of the other classes, these in turn will probably take good care not to come to their assistance, since it is far too much to their interest to maintain the workers in their former state of dependency. Only when this proof has been given, and so given that their competition has made itself felt, only when they have at last met the employers as employers themselves, will their wishes be considered, and will the public support them, more especially the capitalists, who will only then begin to regard them as people who have also to be reckoned with, and who, until then, will regard them as mere ciphers, that, standing alone, count for nothing in the calculation. In the domain of commerce, self-interest, after all, rules supreme, and aims and aspirations, however just and fair in themselves, only then command attention when they have become so powerful that they can force themselves to the front in some irresistibly effective and vigorous form." [1]

---

[1] See Schulze-Delitzsch : " Die Arbeitenden Klassen und das Assoziations Recht in Deutschland " (" The Working-Classes and Co-operation in Germany "). Leipzig, 1858 ; pp. 58, 61, and 63.

Meanwhile, at the Congress of Political Economists in the summer of 1862, Herr Schulze had to admit that so far there were scarcely any productive co-operative societies, and that there were only a very small number of distributive ones. Only the credit and loan societies, composed of manufacturers, small masters, and small business men, flourished, and with these, although in smaller numbers, the raw material co-operative societies.

We have here somewhat anticipated the course of events from 1848 to the beginning of the Lassalle agitation, and now we pick up again the dropped threads.

The Crimean War had already dealt the European reaction a severe blow by seriously shaking that "solidarity of the Powers" which was one of its conditions of existence. The rivalry between Prussia and Austria again became manifest in the different attitudes of their Berlin and Vienna cabinets towards Russia, while the death of Nicolas I., and the position in which the Empire of the Tzar was at the end of the war, deprived the reactionary parties in Europe of their strongest bulwark. The hands of Russia were for the time being so full with its own internal affairs that for years to come it was not in the position to take up the cause of law and order "on principle" in any other country, and for the time being was no longer a factor in the internal policy of the neighbour states. The rivalry between Prussia and Austria was, however, still confined to petty cabinet intrigues, while, so far as their people were concerned, both governments still maintained their "solidarity."

A second blow was dealt the reaction by the general stagnation of trade that began in 1857 or 1858. Just as the general prosperity of 1850 bolstered up the tottering thrones, so the industrial crisis of 1857—greater in extent and intensity than any of its forerunners—again set the thrones tottering. All circles of society suffering through the crisis were in a state of ferment ; everywhere the Opposition found fresh strength in this discontent of the masses ; everywhere the "subversive elements" again reared their head, and most menacingly in France, where, it is true, the throne was least stable. Once more Napoleon III. had recourse to draconic prosecutions, the pretext for them being afforded by the Orsini attempt. But when he found that he was thereby rather weakening than strengthening his position, he had recourse to other methods, and by means of a popular foreign war sought to again consolidate his *régime* at home, and to protect his life against the daggers of the Carbonari. These had, through Orsini, given their quondam fellow-conspirator to understand that if he did not keep his word to them, avengers would again and again arise against him. It was thus the Italian war was inaugurated. Almost at the same time the "new era" began in Prussia with the regency of William I.[1] Dominated by the desire—still kept secret however—of breaking the supremacy of Austria in Germany, William I., then Prince Regent, sought to win over the liberal middle-class, and appointed a ministry agreeable to them.

At first, all went well. Touched at once again having the chance of making themselves heard, and that altogether without effort on its part, middle-class Liberalism surpassed itself in all sorts of protestations of loyalty. The National Union was founded with the programme : Unification of Germany, with Prussia at her head. To Prussia was assigned the honourable part of realising the political and national aspirations of the liberal bourgeoisie. A new spring-time for the people seemed at hand, and a far more beautiful one than that of 1848, for it promised the rose without the thorns. In a revolutionary rising one can never be sure where things are going to stop, or what elements may be let loose in its course. But now there was no need to stir up the unknown masses ; everything promised to come off after the most approved Parliamentary fashion. But if, against all probability, the worst should come to the worst—why, had not the example of the Schulze-Delitzsch provident and distributive societies, his loan and raw material co-operative associations cured the workers of their socialistic Utopias, and given them proof

[1] In the autumn of 1858, the illness of King Frederick William IV. of Prussia—softening of the brain—which had set in in 1857, or even earlier, became so advanced, that he was unable even to sign a decree. As he had no children, his brother William was proclaimed Regent.

positive of the great things they might expect from self-help, convinced them that they wanted nothing, absolutely nothing more than the "liberties" of the Liberals?

Whoever now—thirty years after—re-reads the literature of German Liberalism of those days, is chiefly struck by the colossal *naïveté* predominating in it with regard to all questions that extend beyond the narrow horizon of the enlightened tallow-chandler. They were all very cultured, and very well-read, and they knew all about the ancient Athenian Constitution and English Parliamentary Government. But the practical application drawn from all this was invariably that the enlightened German tallow-chandler or iron-monger was the normal man, and that what was not to his tastes deserved to perish. It was this self-satisfied *naïveté* that forced on the constitutional conflict in the Prussian Parliament, even before they were firm in their saddles ; with this *naïveté* they managed to estrange the working-classes, long before any serious class-differences gave occasion for the estrangement. They knew a terrible lot of history, but they had "learnt" really nothing at all from it.

Then began the constitutional conflict in Prussia. The Government in 1860 proposed a reorganisation of the military system, in accord with its "German policy." The wiseacres of the Landtag, however, instead of either voting or refusing to vote the required supplies, resorted to the expedient of voting them "provisionally" for one year. The Government began the work of reorganisation, and still went on with it, even when a majority of the Landtag, displeased with certain acts and declarations of the king's of rather too arbitrary a nature, subsequently refused to vote fresh supplies.

Liberalism suddenly found itself, not knowing how, involved in a violent dispute with that same Government which it had cast for the fine part of re-establishing the German Empire, and to which it had promised supremacy in Germany. However, this was provisional only—unlucky, but not a misfortune. The Liberal party had, in the meantime, become so strong, it could afford to hold out for a good while. Thanks to the narrow-minded

obstinacy of its opponent, it had well-nigh the whole of the people
at its back. All classes of the population were carried away by
this national movement; all, with the exception of the little
family party of the squirearchy and clericals east of the Elbe, left
it to the then recently constituted Progressist party to fight it out
with the Prussian Government. Whatever mistakes this party
may have made, however heterogeneous its composition, however
inadequate its programme, it represented at that moment—as
against the coalition of landlordism and police absolutism once
again raising its head—a cause whose triumph would be to the
interests of all who did not belong to the feudal elements of
society.

But to entrust a party temporarily with a political mission is
not to give oneself over to it body and soul, not to abjure all independence with regard to it. And this the more advanced German
workers felt. The part of supers which the Liberal leaders expected them to fill; the fare set before them at the educational
and other clubs patronised by these leaders, could not satisfy
them in the long run. The old Communist and revolutionary
traditions had not yet completely died out. There was, indeed,
still many a working-man who had either himself been a member
of one of the Communist Sections, or had been enlightened by
other members as to its principles, and had been supplied by them
with Communist literature. Among these men, and prompted by
them in ever-widening circles of working-men, the question began
to be discussed, whether the time had not come for constituting a
working-men's society, with its own working-men's programme, or,
at least, to create a workers' league, which should be something
more than the mere creature of the Liberal party.

If the gentlemen of the Progressist party and the National
Unionists had only learnt something from the history of other
countries, it would have been an easy matter for them to prevent
this movement from becoming one hostile to themselves, so long as
they were still fighting the Prussian Government. But they were
much—too much—imbued with the conviction that as they represented the people's cause, "the people," especially as "the

people of thinkers," were superior to the narrowness—that is to say the class-struggle—of foreign countries; and thus they failed to see that here also they had to reason with a movement which was bound to set in sooner or later, and that all they had to do was to seek some reasonable way of arriving at a common understanding. But so enamoured were they of themselves, that they were utterly incapable of grasping the idea that the workers could actually want anything further than the honour of being represented by them. The workers asked that the conditions of membership of the National Union should be made easier, and the reply: "All workers might consider honorary membership of the Union as their birthright," *i.e.*, might have the honour to remain outside it—was thoroughly characteristic of the inability of the Schultzes and the rest to understand anything, except the philosophic " shopkeeper,"—their own image, their God.

Thus came about those discussions in the working-men's meetings at Leipzig, which finally resulted in the sending of three delegates to Berlin, and the opening up of negotiations with Ferdinand Lassalle.

CHAPTER II.

WHEN the Leipzig Committee applied to him, Lassalle was in his thirty-seventh year, in the full force of his physical and mental development. He had already lived a strenuous life; he had made himself a name politically and scientifically—both, it is true, within certain limited circles; he was in relations with the most prominent representatives of literature and art; he had ample means and influential friends. In a word, according to ordinary notions, the Committee, composed of hitherto quite unknown men, representing a still embryonic movement, could offer him nothing he did not already possess. Nevertheless, he entered into their wishes with the utmost readiness, and took the initial steps for giving the movement that direction which best accorded with his own views and aims. Quite apart from all other considerations, he must have been particularly attracted by the movement, from the fact that it had as yet taken no definite form, that it offered itself to him as a mass which, without any great difficulty, he could himself mould into shape. First, to give it form, to mould it into an army after his own mind, this not only fell in with his high-soaring plans; it was a task that must have strongly appealed to his natural inclinations. The invitation appealed not merely to his Socialist convictions, but to his weaknesses. And so he accepted it with the greatest readiness.

The present work does not pretend to be an actual "Life" of Ferdinand Lassalle, or to add one more to the very large number of biographies of the founder of the General German Working Men's Association, which, in the space at my disposal, could only be a repetition of oft-told facts. What this work aims at, above

15

all, is to portray the personality and the historical significance of Ferdinand Lassalle, so far as his political, literary, and propagandist work is concerned. Nevertheless, a glance at Lassalle's career is indispensable, since it gives the key to the understanding of his political line of action.

Even his descent appears to have exercised a great, one may even say a fatal influence, upon the development of Lassalle. I am not here speaking of any inherited qualities or inclinations, but simply of the fact that the consciousness that he was of Jewish origin was, according to his own confession, painful to Lassalle even in his more advanced years ; and, despite all his efforts, or perhaps because of these efforts, he never really succeeded in becoming indifferent to his descent, in getting rid of a certain self-conscious awkwardness. But it must not be forgotten that Lassalle was cradled in the eastern part of the Prussian kingdom —he was born at Breslau on the 11th of April, 1825—where, until the year 1843, the Jews were not formally emancipated. Lassalle's father was a wholesale silk merchant, and is described by those who knew him as a very honest, genial, and intelligent man. His mother, on the other hand, appears to have been a somewhat capricious woman, with that love for dress and jewellery so often found in Jewish middle-class women. The wealth of his parents saved Lassalle from many of the miseries under which the poorer Jews had at this time to suffer, but it did not protect him from all sorts of petty mortifications, to which all belonging to an oppressed race, even those in good circumstances, are exposed. And these, in so self-conscious a nature as Lassalle's was from his youth, induce first a defiant fanaticism of revolt, which later not infrequently veers round to its very opposite. How great the fanaticism of the young Lassalle was we see from his " Diary " of the years 1840 and 1841, recently published by Herr Paul Lindau. On the 1st February, 1840, Ferdinand Lassalle, not yet fifteen years old, writes in his diary : . . . " I told him this, and, in fact, I think I am one of the best Jews in existence, although I disregard the Ceremonial Law. I could, like that Jew in Bulwer's ' Leila,' risk my life to deliver the Jews from their present crushing condition. I would not even shrink from the scaffold could I but once more make of them a respected people. Oh! when I yield to my childish dreams, it is ever my favourite fancy to make the Jews armed—I at their head—free." The persecution of the Jews at Damascus, in the May of 1840, drew from him the cry : " A people that bears this is hideous ; let them suffer or avenge this treatment." And to the statement of a reporter : "The Jews of this town endure barbarities such as only these pariahs of the earth would suffer without a horrible reaction," he added the characteristic remark : " Lo, even the Christians marvel at our sluggish blood, that we do not rise, that we do not rather perish on the battlefield than by torture. Was the oppression against which the Swiss one day rebelled greater ? . . . Cowardly people, thou dost merit no better lot." He expresses himself even more passionately a few months later (30th July) : "Again the ridiculous story that Jews make use of Christian blood. The same story at Rhodes and Lemberg as in Damascus. But that this accusation goes forth from all corners of the earth seems to say to me that the time will soon be at hand when we, in very deed, will help ourselves with Christian blood. *Aide toi et le ciel t'aidera.* The dice are ready, it only depends upon the player."

These childish ideas disappear more and more as his views broaden, but the effect of such youthful impressions upon the mind remains. The immediate result was, that the sting of the "tortures" of which he writes, doubly incited the precocious Lassalle to secure recognition and respect for himself at all costs. On the other hand, the rebel against the oppression of the Jews is soon turned into a political revolutionist by the Christians. And yet, after seeing Schiller's " Fiesco," he remarks—showing extraordinarily acute self-criticism : " I know not, although I now have revolutionary-democratic-republican inclinations with the best of them ; yet I feel that in Count Lavagna's place I would have acted just as he did, and would not have contented myself with being Genoa's first citizen, but would rather have stretched forth my hand to the crown. From this it seems, when I look at the matter in the light of day, that I am simply an egotist. Had

I been born prince or ruler I should have been an aristocrat, body
and soul. But now, as I am only a poor burgher's son, I shall be
a democrat in good time."

It was his political radicalism also, which, in 1841, induced the
sixteen-year-old Lassalle to give up the idea, entertained for a time,
of devoting himself to a commercial career, and to get permission
from his father to prepare for the university curriculum. The
generally accepted opinion[1] that Lassalle had been sent to the
Commercial School at Leipzig by his father, against his own will,
has been shown by the diary to be entirely wrong. Lassalle
himself managed his transfer from the Gymnasium to the Commercial School, not, it is true, from any passing predilection for a
business life, but to escape the consequences of a number of
thoughtless escapades, which he had committed in order not to be
obliged to show his father the bad reports which he—in his
opinion, undeservedly—was always receiving. But when he got
on no better at the Leipzig Commercial School than at the
Breslau Gymnasium, when he there too came into conflict with
most of the masters, and especially with the head-master, conflicts
that grew more and more bitter as his opinions became more
radical, Lassalle there and then gave up the idea of a commercial career. In the May of 1840, Lassalle entered the
Commercial School, and already, on the 3rd of August, he
" hopes " that "chance" will one day rescue him from the counting-
house, and throw him upon a stage where he can labour for the
public. " I trust to chance, and to my own strong will to devote
myself more to the muses than to ledgers and journals ; to Hellas

---

[1] A view adopted also by Mr. Dawson in his " German Socialism and
Ferdinand Lassalle." It must, however, be remembered that this book
was written long before the " Diary " had been published. Another story
of Lassalle's youth, that has been repeated by nearly all his biographers, to
the effect that once when a difficulty arose in the family, Lassalle took
matters in hand, and over the heads of father and mother settled the affair,
also finds no confirmation in the " Diary." On the contrary, Lassalle always shows himself most respectful, even submissive, to his father. In the
matter of school certificates, he imitates his mother's signature without a
scruple, but is afraid to do the same with regard to his father's.

and the East than to indigo and beet-root; to Thalia and her priests than to shop-keepers and their clerks; to care more for Freedom than for the price of goods, to execrate more deeply those dogs of aristocrats, who rob man of his first and highest possession, than the rival competitors who bring down prices." And he adds : " But I shall not content myself with execrations." And with this Radicalism there grew in him an ever stronger longing to shake off the Jew in him, a longing which at last becomes so overwhelming that when Lassalle informed his father in May, 1841, of his " irrevocable" determination to go to the university after all, he at the same time refused to study medicine or law, for " the doctor and the lawyer are both tradesmen who traffic with their knowledge." He would study " for the sake of what can be done with knowledge." The father, it is true, did not acquiesce in this last idea, but nevertheless consented to Lassalle's preparing for a university career.

Lassalle now worked with such desperate energy, that, in 1842, he was already able to pass his matriculation examination. He began by studying philology, then turned to philosophy, and sketched the outline of a great philologico-philosophical work, on the Philosopher Heraclitus of Ephesus. That he should have chosen this thinker of all others as the subject for his researches—a thinker whom the greatest Greek philosophers themselves admitted they could never feel sure of understanding rightly, and who was therefore called the " Dark "—is strikingly characteristic of Lassalle. And what attracted Lassalle even more than the teaching of Heraclitus, whom Hegel himself had acknowledged as his forerunner, was the conviction that here only by brilliant achievement could laurels be won. And with this longing to dazzle all men by some extraordinary achievement, already referred to, Lassalle was convinced that he was equal to any task he might set himself. This boundless self-confidence was the bane of his life. It helped him, indeed, to undertake, and to carry through, things from which thousands, even though endowed with Lassalle's intellectual gifts, would have shrunk; but, on the other hand, it was the cause of many fatal mistakes, and finally of his unhappy end.

After completing his course of studies, Lassalle went, in 1844, to the Rhine, and later to Paris, partly in order to work at the libraries there, partly in order to see the world-city, the centre of the intellectual life of the time. The tide of the socialist movement was running very high in Paris at this moment, and it is probable that here Lassalle found his socialist Damascus. Whether, or to what extent, Lassalle became acquainted with the German socialists living in Paris—Karl Marx, after the " Deutsch-französischen Jahrbücher " had gone under, and the " Vorwärts " was suspended, had been expelled from Paris, and had migrated to Brussels, in January, 1845—on this point we have no reliable information. But on the other hand it is known that he associated much with Heinrich Heine, to whom he had an introduction, and to whom he rendered the greatest services in an unpleasant money transaction, (a disputed inheritance). The letters in which the sick poet expressed his gratitude and admiration for the twenty-year-old Lassalle are well-known, and as they are quoted in Mr. Dawson's work,[1] may here be omitted.

Having returned to Germany, Lassalle, in 1846, made the acquaintance of the Countess Hatzfeld. For years the Countess had been trying to obtain a judicial separation, and the restitution of her fortune, from her husband, Count Hatzfeld, who had subjected her to the grossest ill-usage and insults. The whole case affords a curious illustration of the habits of the German aristocracy before the Revolution of 1848. Though not a lawyer, Lassalle took it upon himself to conduct the Countess' case. It was an extraordinary undertaking, requiring all the skill, astuteness, and acumen of an experienced lawyer. But if Lassalle could not bring to the work the advantage of experience, he brought, besides his rare intellectual gifts, the zeal, the devotion, the audacity, and the pertinacity of youth, and with these succeeded where probably the most eminent lawyer would have failed. The warfare between Lassalle and Count Hatzfeld lasted for years. Its most famous incident was the oft-told story of the " casket-robbery."

One fine day Count Hatzfeld attempted, in the form of a loan,

[1] Pages 115-117.

to make over the whole of the fortune of his second son, Paul—whom he hated, because the boy had remained with his mother—to one of his mistresses, a certain Baroness von Meyendorff. The affair was discovered, and the Count, caught in the act of perpetrating this fraud, promised to cancel the deed of gift. But he did this simply to gain time. A few days later he refused all further negotiations, and the Baroness von Meyendorff secretly left the place, taking with her a casket, supposed to contain the deed of gift. Lassalle immediately induced two of his friends—both rich, and one himself a judge—to follow the Baroness, and to ascertain, at all costs, whether she was in possession of the document, or whether the deed of gift had been cancelled. They ran her down at Cologne, and by unexpected luck for a while obtained possession of the casket, but failed to retain possession of it. They were subsequently arrested, and—such a lottery is justice! while he who had seized the casket—the judge—was acquitted, the man to whom he handed it over—a physician—was condemned to five years' penal servitude. Lassalle, though a younger man than either of the others, was prosecuted for " inciting to the theft of a casket." Fortunately, he was tried by jury, in August, 1848, when the Revolution of March, in the same year, had somewhat altered the state of things in Germany. After a seven days' trial, at the end of which Lassalle spoke for six hours—(the " Casket Speech ")—the jury dismissed the charge.

It is interesting to note that the young Count Paul Hatzfeld referred to is the present Ambassador from the German Empire to the Court of St. James's.

There has been much speculation on the motives which induced Lassalle to take the Countess' case in hand. Some have explained them by a love affair with the no longer youthful, but still very beautiful, woman, whilst Lassalle himself, at the " Casket Trial," passionately protested that his sole motive had been one of pity for a persecuted woman, deserted by her friends, the victim of her social position, the object of the brutal persecution of an insolent aristocrat. There is absolutely no reason for refusing to believe this statement of Lassalle's. Whether

Lassalle did not for a time enter into closer relationship than that of friendship with her in later years we cannot say. But even on purely psychological grounds, it is improbable that such a relationship should have existed at the beginning of their acquaintance, when Lassalle took up the lawsuit. It is far more probable that, in addition to his perhaps somewhat romantic and exaggerated, yet most worthy partisanship of a persecuted woman and hatred of the great aristocrat, Lassalle was attracted by the fact that here was an affair which only the use of extraordinary measures, and the display of extraordinary energy, could bring to a successful issue. What would have repelled others, unquestionably attracted him.

He came out of the lawsuit victorious; he had the triumphant satisfaction of seeing the insolent aristocrat forced to capitulate to him, the " stupid Jew boy." But he did not come out of the struggle scatheless. To win it he had certainly been obliged to resort to extraordinary measures. But it was not, or rather it was not merely, a matter of extraordinary grasp of the legal issues, of extraordinary readiness and dexterity in parrying the enemy's thrusts. There were also the extraordinary measures of underground warfare ; the spying, the bribery, the burrowing in the nastiest scandal and filth.[1] Count Hatzfeld, a coarse sensualist, stuck at nothing to attain his ends, and in order to thwart his dirty manœuvres, the other side resorted to means that were not much more clean. No one who has not read the documents of the case can have any conception of the filth raked up, and again and again dragged forward, of the nature of the accusations on both sides, and the witnesses. And the after effects of his inverted Augean labours in the Hatzfeld Trial Lassalle never quite shook off.

I do not say this from the point of view of Philistine morality, or in reference to his later love affairs. I refer rather

---

[1] Thus, a printed document of over seventy large quarto pages contains nothing but the enumeration of Count Hatzfeld's misconduct with women of all classes. It is impossible to imagine more disgusting reading than this,

to his readiness, henceforth again and again manifested, to welcome and to make use of any means that seemed likely to further
the ends he had, for the time being, in view ; I refer to the loss
of that feeling of tact which forbids a man of convictions, even in
the thick of a violent struggle, to take any step opposed to the
principles he represents ; I refer to that loss of good taste, that
want of moral judgment, henceforth so often shown and most
strongly marked during the tragic closing episode of his life. It
was as a youthful enthusiast that Lassalle had plunged into the
Hatzfeld Case. In his "Casket Speech," he himself uses the
image of the swimmer :—"What man, being a strong swimmer,
could see another swept away by the stream without going to his
aid ? Well, I considered myself a good swimmer, I was free, and
so I plunged into the stream." True, no doubt, but the stream
into which he plunged was a very muddy one, a stream that
ended in a vast quagmire. And when Lassalle emerged from it
he had been infected by the rottenness of the society with which
he had had to deal. For a long time his originally finer instincts
struggled against the effects of this poison, often successfully
beating them back, but finally he after all succumbed.

What I have said may to some seem too severe, but we shall
see in the course of this study that it is only just to Lassalle. It
is not for me to write an apology, but rather to give a critical
representation, and for this the first requisite is to explain the
effects by the causes.

Before proceeding further, however, we must first consider
the part played by Lassalle in 1848.

On the outbreak of the Revolution of March, Lassalle was so
deeply entangled in the meshes of the Hatzfeld Case that he had
at the beginning almost condemned himself to political inaction.
In the August of 1848 he was tried for " inciting to the theft of
a Casket," and his hands were full preparing for the trial. It
was only after his acquittal that he again found leisure to take a
direct part in the political events of this stirring time.

Lassalle, who was then living at Düsseldorf—the birthplace of
Heine,—as Republican and Socialist, of course was on the extreme

left of the Democratic party, whose organ was the *Neue Rheinische Zeitung* (the New Rhenish Gazette), edited by Karl Marx. Karl Marx had, moreover, for a time been a member of the District Committee of the Rhenish Democrats, whose headquarters were Cologne.[1] A double opportunity was thus given Lassalle for bringing him into closer relations with Marx. He communicated by word of mouth and by letter with the District Committee mentioned above, he frequently sent communications and correspondence to the *Neue Rheinische Zeitung*, and occasionally even appeared at the editorial office of the paper. Thus, gradually, a friendly personal relation came about between Lassalle and Marx, and this later, when Marx was living in exile, was kept up by letters, and now and again by visits. Lassalle frequently came to London, while Marx, during a journey to Germany, in 1861, visited Lassalle in Berlin. Nevertheless, there never at any time existed any deeper friendship between the two ; for this their natures were far too diverse. Other matters that stood in the way of any intimacy beyond comradeship in the political fight will be discussed later on.

Lassalle's attitude with regard to the inflowing tide of reaction in 1848 was identical with that of the editors of the *Neue Rheinische Zeitung*, and of the party at the back of them. When, in November, 1848, the Prussian Government disbanded the

---

1 Mr. Dawson is not quite accurate when he says that Marx, Engels, and Wolff "saw in the foment of that period an opportunity for furthering their long-cherished Communistic designs." The authors of the "Communist Manifesto" and their friends recognised clearly that before they could do this they must further the political revolution in Germany. In accordance with the principles enunciated in the Manifesto, they supported the most advanced and the most resolute wing of the Radical Middle-Class party. The *Neue Rheinische Zeitung* pointed out their duty to the German middle-classes, while, at the same time, it answered the treachery and cowardice of the so-called "moderates," and denounced the proceedings of the Reactionary Government. No Socialist or Communist "scheme" was ever propounded in the *Neue Rheinische Zeitung*, and the Socialist principles of the editors found expression only in articles like that of Marx on the June Revolution in Paris, or in the publication of Karl Marx' lecture on "Wage-labour and Capital."

Berlin civic guard, proclaimed a state of siege in Berlin, and removed the seat of the National Assembly from Berlin to Brandenburg, a small provincial town, and when in time the National Assembly impeached the Prussian Ministry for high treason (*i.e.*, violation of the Constitution), and declared this ministry had forfeited the right of levying taxes, Lassalle, following the example of the *Neue Rheinische Zeitung*, called upon all citizens to organise and offer an armed resistance to the collection of taxes. Like the Committee of the Rhenish Democrats, Lassalle was also indicted for inciting to armed resistance against the King's authority, and like them, too, he was acquitted by the jury. But the Reaction, growing more and more high-handed, brought a further charge against Lassalle of inciting to resistance against Government officials, with the object of getting him tried before the Correctional Police Court. And, in fact, this court—the Government undoubtedly knew its own judges—eventually did condemn Lassalle to six months' imprisonment.

Lassalle's answer to the first of these charges has been published under the title "Assize Court Speech" ("*Assisen-Rede*"). But, as a matter of fact, it was never really spoken, and everything that has been said in the various biographies of the "profound" impression it produced upon the jury and the public therefore belongs to the domain of fable. Even before the trial came on, Lassalle had sent the speech to the printer's, and as some complete proofs had also been circulated beforehand, the court decided to exclude the public. When, in spite of Lassalle's protest, and his declaration that the proofs had been circulated without his knowledge, and very probably at the instigation of, and through bribery by, his enemies, the court decided to maintain its decision, and thereupon Lassalle declined to defend himself, but was none the less acquitted.

Whether spoken or not, the Assize Court Speech, in any case, is an interesting document for the study of Lassalle's political development. In it he takes almost the same standpoint as that taken three months earlier by Marx in his speech to the Cologne Jury.[1] A comparison of the two speeches demonstrates this as

[1] On the 9th February, 1849, Marx, together with Karl Schapper and

clearly as it demonstrates the difference of the natures of Marx and Lassalle. Marx refrains from all oratorical flourish ; he goes straight to the point, in simple and terse language ; sentence by sentence he develops incisively, and with ruthless logic, his own standpoint, and, without any peroration, ends with a summary of the political situation. Anyone would think that Marx' own personality was in no wise concerned, and that his only business was to deliver a political lecture to the jury. And, in fact, at the end of the trial, one of the jurors went to Marx to thank him, in the name of his colleagues, for the very instructive lecture he had given them ! Lassalle's peroration, on the other hand, lasts almost from beginning to end ; he exhausts himself in images— often very beautiful—and superlatives. It is all sentiment, and whether he refers to the cause he represented or to himself, he never speaks to the jury, but to the gallery, to an imaginary mass meeting, and after declaring a vengeance that should be "as

the solicitor Schneider, was tried for "inciting the people to armed resistance against the Government and its officials," by publishing, on November 18th, 1848, in the name of the Provincial Committee of the Rhenish Democrats, the following proclamation :—

The Provincial Committee of Rhenish Democrats calls upon all democratic associations of the Rhenish Provinces to secure the acceptation and execution of the following measures :

(1) The Prussian National Assembly having itself refused to vote the taxes, all attempts to collect such taxes by force are to be resisted in every way.

(2) The " Landsturm " (armed men) are everywhere to be organised for resisting the enemy. Those without means are to be supplied with arms and amunition by the municipalities, or by voluntary contributions.

(3) The authorities everywhere to be called upon to declare publicly whether they intend to acknowledge and carry out the wishes of the National Assembly.

In the event of their refusing to do this, committees of public safety to be formed, whenever possible, in conjunction with the municipalities. Any municipality opposing the Legislative Assembly to be replaced by a new one duly elected.

After a masterly speech by Marx, and short addresses by Schapper and Schneider, the three were acquitted, although they had declared that by "the enemy" they meant the armed forces of the Government. (See "Karl Marx vor den Kölner Geschwornen," Zürich, 1885.)

tremendous " as " the insult offered the people," he ended with a
recitation from Schiller's Tell.

Even when in prison, where, by his energy and pertinacity,
Lassalle obtained privileges not usually granted prisoners—thus
he frequently received permission, a proceeding he himself later on
declared illegal, to plead in the Countess Hatzfeld's law suits—and
for many years after this, Lassalle's energies were almost wholly
absorbed by the Hatzfeld affair. Besides this, Lassalle kept open
house for his political friends, and for a long time gathered around
him a circle of advanced working-men, to whom he delivered
political lectures. At last, in 1854, the Hatzfeld case came to an
end. The Countess received a considerable fortune, and Lassalle
was assured a yearly income of 7000 thalers (£1050), which
allowed him to order his way of life after his own heart.

For the time being Lassalle continued to reside at Düsseldorf,
and here worked on at his " Heraclitus." Moreover, he undertook
all sorts of journeys, among others, one to the East. But in the long
run, not even these could reconcile him to residing in a provincial
town, where all political life had died out. He longed for a freer,
more stimulating life than the Rhenish town could offer or permit
him, for intercourse with notable personalities, and for a wider
sphere of action. And so, in 1827, he managed to obtain, through
the instrumentality of Alexander von Humboldt, permission from
the King of Prussia to take up his abode in Berlin.

His petition, as well as the permission granted, deserve notice.
In May, 1849, Lassalle had branded in burning words the " shameful and insufferable Government by force that had burst forth in
Prussia ; " he had cried aloud : " Why with so much force is there
so much hypocrisy? But that is Prussian," and " Let us forget
nothing, never, never. . . Let us cherish these remembrances
carefully, as the ashes of murdered parents, the sole heritage from
whom is the oath of vengeance bound up with these ashes." (Assize-
Court Speech). After taking up this attitude, it must assuredly
have required a good deal of self-abnegation to address such a
petition to the very Government which had been attacked in this
way, and to appeal to that Government's good-will in order to obtain

it. Lassalle must have been desperately anxious to live in the Prussian capital, and one can hardly wonder if this step of his met with the disapproval of some of his political friends. Lassalle, who could be very rigorous towards others, and who, *e.g.*, many years later urged Marx to give up all intercourse with Liebknecht, because the latter was at that time the correspondent of the *Augsburger Allgemeine Zeitung,* applied a different rule where he was himself concerned. He was thirsting for recognition, for fame, for action, and for these the capital itself was necessary.

Nor is it impossible that Lassalle had been informed, through the relations of the Countess Hatzfeld, which were pretty far-reaching, that a new wind was about to blow in the higher circles of Prussia. How far-reaching these relations were, is shown by the information which Lassalle sent to Marx in London on the outbreak of the Crimean War in 1854. Thus, on the 10th February 1854, he forwards Marx the text of the declaration sent, a few days before, by the Berlin Cabinet to Paris and to London, and describes the situation in the Berlin Cabinet—the King and almost the whole Cabinet for Russia, only Manteuffel and the Crown Prince of Prussia for England—and the measures decided upon by it in the event of certain contingencies. Upon this he writes : " You can look upon all the news sent herewith as if you had it from Manteuffel's or Aberdeen's own lips ! "

Four weeks later he again sent all kinds of information about the steps the Cabinet contemplated taking, based upon information received, " not, it is true, from my ' official ' source, but still from a fairly reliable one." On the 20th May, 1854, he deplores that his " diplomatic informant " had started on a long journey. " To have so excellent a source of information that kept one informed as if one had been in the Cabinet, and then to lose it again for so long a time is exceedingly annoying." But he still has other sources of information that keep him posted as to the internal movements of the Berlin Cabinet, and so, among other things he had received early information of Bonin's dismissal, etc.

Some of these " informants " were very closely connected with the Berlin Court, and their reports may have induced Lassalle to take the step he did. The mental alienation of Frederick William IV. was at this time already very far advanced, and even though the faithful ministers and the guardians of the monarchical idea did not yet think it advanced enough to declare the King incapable of reigning, yet everyone in well-informed circles knew that the Regency of the Prince of Prussia was now only a question of months.

At Berlin, Lassalle now completed his "Heraclitus," which was published at the end of 1857, by Franz Duncker. Authorities differ as to the value of this work. Some regard it as epoch-making ; others declare that in all essentials it contains nothing Hegel had not already said. Certain it is, that here Lassalle almost throughout his work accepts the old Hegelian standpoint. Things are developed from ideas, categories of thought are treated as eternal metaphysical entities, whose movement begets history. But even those who question the epoch-making character of Lassalle's work, admit that it is a very notable achievement. It gave Lassalle an honoured name in the scientific world.

But as characteristic of Lassalle and his mental development, "The Philosophy of Heraclitus the Dark of Ephesus," is not simply noticeable because it shows us Lassalle as a determined disciple of Hegel. Herein we agree with the well-known Danish literary historian, G. Brandes, when in his study[1] of Lassalle—a work that often deals pretty freely with facts for the sake of literary effect—he says that various passages in the work on "Heraclitus" supply the key for the understanding of Lassalle's view of life. This, of course, applies especially to Lassalle's cult of the idea of the State—in this, too, Lassalle was an old Hegelian—and to his conception of honour and of fame. With regard to the former, Brandes says :

"The ethic of Heraclitus," Lassalle says (Vol. II. p. 431), "is summed up in the one idea, which is also the eternal fundamental concept of the moral itself : 'devotion to universality.'" This is at once Greek and modern ; but Lassalle cannot

[1] Ferdinand Lassalle, "Ein literarisches Charaterbild." Berlin, 1877. G. Brandes.

resist the temptation of demonstrating in his working-out of this idea by the old Greeks that they were in accord with Hegel's philosophy of the State (Vol. II. p. 439). " As in the Hegelian philosophy laws also are conceived as the realisation of the universal actual Will, while this conception is not for a moment considered in relation to the formal Will of the individuals and their enumeration, so is the universality of Heraclitus equally removed from the category of empirical totality."

Nor was Brandes wrong when he recognised a contradiction between this conception of the State, that recurs again and again in Lassalle, and his confession of democratic faith and belief in universal suffrage, which, after all, expresses the rule of " the formal will and of the individual," a contradiction " no one can harbour in his mind without taint." In the domain of principle it is, he says, the counterpart to that contrast which " expressed itself outwardly when Lassalle with his studiously elegant dress, and studiously fine linen, and his patent leather boots, addressed a circle of sooty-faced and horny-handed factory workers." [1]

This is expressed in the terms of the *littérateur.* As a matter of fact, Lassalle's old Hegelian state-concept led him, in his subsequent struggle with the Manchester school, to overshoot the mark.

As to Lassalle's conception of honour and fame, Brandes says : " Another point of similarity, the last between Heraclitus and Lassalle, is the passionate desire, despite all self-sufficiency and pride, for fame and honour, for the admiration and the praise of others." Heraclitus has enunciated the oft-quoted axiom (Vol. II. p. 434): "The greater destinies achieve the greater fate." And he has said, throwing the true light upon this saying (Vol. II. p. 436): " That the masses, and those who deem themselves wise, follow the singers of the people, and seek counsel from the laws, not knowing that the masses are bad, a few only good ; but the best follow after fame. For," he adds, " the best ever seek one thing rather than everything, the everlasting fame of mortals." So fame was for Heraclitus identical with that greater lot, which

[1] Brandes : p. 42.

the greater destinies achieve; his striving after honour was not merely the immediate striving that is in the blood, but one based upon reflection and philosophy. "Fame," says Lassalle, "is, in fact, the antithesis to everything, the antithesis to the categories of immediate, actual Being as a whole, and of its individual aims. It is the Being of man in his non-being, a continuance in the decay of sentient existence itself; it is therefore the immortality of man attained and made real." And he adds with warmth : "Just as this is the reason why fame has always so mightily stirred the great souls and lifted them beyond all petty and narrow ends, it is the reason why Platen, singing of it, says it can only be attained 'hand in hand with the all-testing Angel of Death,' so also is it the reason why Heraclitus recognised in it the ethic realisation of his speculative principle " (p. 45).

Truly it was not in Lassalle's nature to content himself with the fame that is only to be attained hand in hand with the Angel of Death. In contrast with the Heraclitean contempt for the masses, he thirsted for their applause, and with the utmost self-complacency took any sign that seemed to promise him this, no matter how insignificant, for the applause itself. The predilection for the sentimental, which was so very marked in Lassalle, usually implies cynicism and hypocrisy. Now if Lassalle cannot be altogether acquitted of having had a certain amount of the former, no one can accuse him of ever making any secret of that which Brandes calls "his unfortunate fondness for the noise and the drum-beating of Fame, and for the blare of its trumpets." In his writings, in his speeches, in his letters, it is displayed with a frankness, whose *naïveté* to some extent disarms one. When Helene von Rakowitza in her " Apology " says that Lassalle pictured to her at Berne how he should one day, as the people's chosen President of the Republic, make his entry into Berlin " drawn by six white steeds," one is tempted either to believe that the authoress is exaggerating, or to assume that Lassalle hoped by picturing so enticing a future to obtain a firmer hold upon the heart of his lady-love. However, the well-known " Soul's Confession," written to Sophie von Solutzew, proves that this picture of the future was by no means the sport of an idle hour, or a lover's fancy, but that it was an idea with which Lassalle intoxicated himself, whose magic exercised a mighty charm upon him. He calls himself—in 1860—" the head of a party," with regard to which " almost our whole Society " has divided into two parties : the one—a portion of the bourgeoisie and the people—" respect, love, aye, not infrequently, honour " Lassalle, for it he is " a man of the greatest genius, and of almost superhuman character, of whom they expect the greatest deeds." The other party—the whole of the aristocracy and the greater portion of the bourgeoisie —fear him " more than anyone else, and therefore hate him ' indescribably.' " If the women of this aristocratic society will not forgive Sophie von Solutzew for marrying such a man, on the other hand, many women will not forgive her because such a man has married her, " will envy her a good fortune that is beyond her deserts. And truly, I will not conceal from you, that, if certain events come about, it might well be that a flood of action, sonorous and splendid, would burst upon your life, should you become my wife."

Exaggerated as all these utterances appear, little as they all corresponded to the actual facts, at a time when there was no thought of a Social Democratic party, and when indeed Lassalle was socially on the best of terms with the middle-class Liberals and Democrats, and had just published a pamphlet that was, in the main, at one with the aspirations of the Prussian Cabinet, they yet contain a great subjective truth : Lassalle himself believed in them. Lassalle believed in the party that acknowledged him as its head, even though that party for the time being consisted of himself alone, and though even in his own ideas it was yet of the vaguest. The party was HIMSELF—HIS aims, and HIS plans. Every word of recognition from his friends, or from those he took for friends, was a confirmation of his mission, every clever piece of flattery, frank homage. Marvellous are the contradictions of which human nature is capable ! Lassalle, as we know from his intimate acquaintances, and as we can see from his letters, was extremely lavish of flattering adjectives ; but when he used them himself they were to him only worthless dross; when applied to him by others he took them for pure gold.

So interwoven was his party with himself in his own imagination, that when later he really did stand at the head of a party, or, at any rate, at the head of a party that was in course of formation, he could only regard it from the point of view of his own personality, and treated it accordingly. Let me not be misunderstood. It is absurd to say that Lassalle created the General German Workingmen's Association only to serve his own ambition; that Socialism was to him only a means, not an end. Lassalle was a convinced Socialist. Of this there can be no doubt. But he would have been incapable of sinking himself in the Socialist movement, of sacrificing his personality—note that we do not say his life—to it.

So much on this matter for the present. The Greek philosopher was followed by a German knight. Shortly after the "Heraclitus" had appeared, Lassalle completed a historical drama that he had already sketched out at Düsseldorf. This, after an arrangement of it for the stage anonymously sent in had been refused by the manager of the Royal Theatre, he published under his own name in 1859. It was called "Franz von Sickingen, a Historical Tragedy." That the play was unsuited to the stage Lassalle himself subsequently admitted, and he attributed this chiefly to its dearth of poetical imagination. As a matter of fact, the drama, in spite of some most effective scenes, and pregnant language, gives on the whole an impression of dryness; its tendency is too obtrusive, there is too much reflection in it, and above all, there are too many speeches. The metre also is extraordinarily awkward. Brandes says that a friend of Lassalle's, whom, whilst working at "Franz von Sickingen," he asked for advice, and who had been a skilled versifier, told Lassalle he had better write the play in prose, and I agree with Brandes that better advice could not have been given. For Lassalle's prose really has many excellent qualities, and even the strongly-marked tendency to drop into declamation would not have mattered in a drama like "Sickingen." But Lassalle was not to be dissuaded from his idea that the metrical form was indispensable for the drama, and so not only his knights and heroes halt along on the most turgid of five-footed iambics, but even the insurgent peasants strut on the stilts of blank verse. The only exception is in the well-known riddle :

> " Loset, sagt an : Was ist das für ein Wesen ?
> Wir können von Pfaffen und Adel nicht genesen." [1]

And the effect is really refreshing.

However, these technical questions are of less moment for us than the subject-matter and the tendency of the drama. In " Franz von Sickingen," Lassalle wanted to improve upon the historical drama as created by Schiller and Goethe ; to go a step further. The historical struggle was not, as is especially the case with Schiller, merely to supply the background for the tragic conflict, while the real dramatic action is concerned only with purely individual interests and destinies. The historical conditions of the times and of the people were to be the actual subject of the tragedy, so that this should not concern itself with individuals as such, individuals who are but the representatives and embodiment of the conflicting interests, but with the greatest and most potent destinies of nations—" destinies which determine the weal or woe of the general spirit of the time, and which are made by the dramatis personæ with the consuming passions begotten of historic aims, the one question of their life." " And with all that it is possible," Lassalle thinks, " to endow these characters, out of the clearness of thought and aim which is theirs, with definite, firm, and even pronounced and realistic individuality." (See Preface to " Franz von Sickingen.") If, and to what extent Lassalle solved the problem he had set himself, how far the problem is solvable at all, under what conditions the great struggles of humanity and of the peoples can be thus embodied in individuals in such a way that neither the one side

---

[1] " Hear ! what species of existence this ?
For priests and lords we cannot live."

nor the other, neither the great and vast significance of those struggles, nor the living personality of the individuals should be unduly neglected, are questions which must here be left untouched. Suffice it to say that Lassalle, in working out his drama, started with this theory. And now as to the drama itself.

As its title indicates, its central idea is the struggle of Franz von Sickingen against the German princes. Sickingen, a Franconian nobleman, was one of those nobles who, at the time of the Reformation, stood out not only against the princes of the various German states, but also against the rule of the Church of Rome in Germany. Sickingen towered above others of his class by his moral and intellectual qualities, his military capacity, his broad views, and his readiness to succour the oppressed. Together with his learned, and even more enthusiastic friend, Ulrich von Hutten, he attempted to bring about a revolutionary movement, with the object of restoring to the German Empire its past glory, but freed from the influence of Rome. But their efforts failed. The burghers in the towns and the peasants in the country had no confidence in the nobles, while most of the latter deserted their leaders. Sickingen was defeated by the superior armies of the princes, and fell, mortally wounded, at Landsthul in 1523. Hutten was forced to fly to Switzerland, where he died, in poverty, at the little island of Utnau, on the Lake of Zürich. This truly remarkable man, Franz von Sickingen, and his friend and adviser, Ulrich von Hutten, are the heroes of the drama, and it is difficult to say which of the two, the military man and statesman, or the representative of the views of the small German nobility, is the more interesting. Oddly enough, Lassalle attempted to paint himself, not in the former, but in the latter. "Read my tragedy,' he writes to Sophie von Solutzew ; " everything I could say to you here, I have made Hutten say. He too had to bear all kinds of calumny, every form of hatred, every species of malevolence. I have made of him the mirror of my soul, and I was able to do this as his fate and my own are absolutely identical, and of astounding similarity." It would have been difficult even for Lassalle to prove this astounding similarity, especially at the time when he wrote this letter. He was leading a luxurious life in Berlin; he associated with members of all circles of the well-to-do classes, and as a politician was very far from being hated in the same way as was the Franconian knight, the inspirer of the passionate polemical pamphlets against the sway of the Romish priests. Only in a few external points can we find any analogy between Lassalle and Hutten. In this case, however, the actual facts are of less importance than what Lassalle himself believed, and what inspired his work. People of such enormous self-sufficiency are, as a rule, easily deceived about themselves. Enough that we have before us, in the Hutten of the play, Lassalle as he was thinking at that time; and the speeches he puts in the mouth of Hutten thus acquire a special value for the understanding of the Lassallean range of ideas.

Here we may chiefly note Hutten's answer to the doubts of Oekolampadius as to the proposed rising :

> " Most honoured sir ! you know not history well.
> You are quite right, and reason is its theme."[1]

A thoroughly Hegelian phrase.

> " And still its form remains for ever Force."

And then when Oekolampadius has spoken of the " profanation of the teaching of Love by the sword " :

> " Most honoured sir ! think better of the sword !
> A sword that's lifted high for Freedom is
> The Word made flesh, the Word of which you preach,
> The God, in very truth, new-born to us.
> By sword our Christianity was spread ;
> By sword was Deutschland baptized by that Carl,
> Whom w to-day, still wondering, call the Great.
> And by the sword was heathendom o'erthrown,
> And by the sword the Saviour's grave was freed !
> It was the sword drove Tarquin out of Rome ;

---

[1] In translating the verse we have adhered as literally as possible to the original, and have tried to put it in metrical form. *(Translator.)*

It was the sword whipped Xerxes home from Greece,
And Science and the Arts were born to us.
With sword smote David, Samson, Gideon.
So now as ever has the sword achieved
The noble things that History has seen;
And all things great that ever will be done
Will owe all their success unto the sword."

No doubt there was a great deal of exaggeration in the lines : "And still "—*i.e.*, History's—"form still remains for ever Force," "and all things great that ever will be done, will owe all their success unto the sword." Nevertheless, the statement that the sword that's lifted high for Freedom is the "Word made flesh," that whosoever would attain Freedom, must be prepared to fight for it with the sword, was fully justified at a time when large numbers in the circles of the *ci-devant* democracy were becoming more and more inclined to expect everything from the power of the Word. Very timely, too, and not only for that particular period are the words Lassalle makes Balthasar Schlör speak to Sickingen in the last act :

"Oh, not the first are you, nor yet will be
The last of those men doomed to lose their heads
By cunningness in great affairs. Disguise
Upon the mart of history counts nought.
Where in the whirl the people recognise
Thee only by thy armour and thy badge ;
So always clothe thyself from top to toe
With boldness ; wear the hue of thine own flag.
So canst thou prove in the colossal strife
The motive power of thy foundation sure,
And thou dost stand and fall with thy whole will."

And Sickingen's words :

"Show not the end and aim, but show the way,
For here so intermingle way and end
That one still changes with the other's change,
And other ways lead still to other ends."

are a phrase from Lassalle's own political confession of faith. Unfortunately, however, he disregarded it exactly at the most critical period of his political career.

But we will not dwell upon isolated passages; rather let us consider the drama as a whole, get at the quintessence of it.

The part actually played in history by Hutten and Sickingen was an entirely different one from what they thought or meant it to be. Both were representatives of the feudal knights, a class, at the time of the Reformation, in its period of decadence. What they wished to do was to stop this process of decay, an idle effort, inevitably doomed to failure, and that only expedited what it meant to stave off. As Hutten and Sickingen by character and by intellect towered high above their class, we here certainly have the making of a true tragedy—the hopeless struggle of strong personalities fighting against historical necessity. This aspect of the Hutten-Sickingen movement is, oddly enough, ignored in Lassalle's drama, despite its great significance to—I will not say Socialists alone—but even to the modern, scientific conception of history. In the play the efforts of Hutten-Sickingen fail, because of a mass of fortuitous circumstances—want of forethought, error of judgment, treachery, etc. And Hutten-Lassalle concludes with the words : " To future ages I bequeath an avenging." This involuntarily reminds one of the thoroughly unhistorical conclusion of Götz von Berlichingen : [1] " Woe to the century that rejected thee ! Woe to the future generations that deny thee ! " But if we can understand why the youthful Goethe, in the eighteenth century, could choose for his hero a representative of this decadent knighthood, it is more difficult to understand how, almost a century later, and at a time when historical research had opened up quite different views for understanding the struggles of the Reformation-period, a Socialist like Lassalle could choose two representatives of that very knighthood as the standard-bearers " of a historico-social process," upon the result of which, as Lassalle says in his pre-

---

[1] A youthful drama of Goethe. Götz von Berlichingen was a Suabian knight, and he too rebelled against the German Princes. But he represents a type infinitely inferior to that of Hutten and Sickingen.

face, "our whole actual society depends." "I wished, if possible," he adds in the same preface, " to make this process of historical development once again pulsate consciously and with quivering passion through the veins of the people. The power to attain such an end is only given to poetry, and so I determined to write this drama."

Now, it is true that besides representing the cause of Knighthood, Hutten and Sickingen also represent the struggle against the supremacy of Rome, and for the unity of the Empire ; two demands which, while ideologically those of the decaying Knighthood, were historically in the interest of the rising bourgeoisie. And thus, when Germany has developed, and has recovered from the immediate effects of the Thirty Years' War, they again come to the front, and in the nineteenth century were championed above all others by the Liberal middle-class. It was only after the establishment of the new German Empire that the German nobility remembered it had once produced so respectable a person as Franz von Sickingen—Hutten it cannot stomach even yet. In the fifties, and even later, " Gartenlaube Liberalism " [1] honoured Hutten and Sickingen as the advanced guard of the national and advanced movement, and ignored their efforts on behalf of their class. And Lassalle does exactly the same in his drama. Ulrich von Hutten and Franz von Sickingen fight against the Roman Antichrist solely for the sake of intellectual freedom ; against the princes only in the interest of the national cause. " What we desire," says Sickingen, in his dialogue with Hutten,

> " That is a single Deutschland, mighty, great,
> A shattering of all government by priests,
> A final breaking with all Roman ways,
> Pure teaching that is Deutschland's only church,
> A new birth quite commensurate with the old,
> Of old Germania's common liberty ;
> Complete destruction of our Princelings' sway
> And of the rule by middlemen usurped,
> And mighty stress and strain of time,

[1] " Gartenlaube " is the German equivalent of our " Mrs. Grundy."

> Firm based and deeply rooted in her soul
> One evangelic chief as Kaiser at the head
> Of the great realm,"

And Hutten answers, " True is the picture."

In fact it is less true than analogous. It fits in wonderfully— since it ignores the aims which Hutten and Sickingen pursued besides fighting against Rome and the princes, and for the " timely " new birth of old Germanic freedom — with a pro- gramme which, over three hundred years later, became the watch- word of Kleindeutsch [1] Liberalism; it breathes the spirit of the approaching Prussian "new era."

As Lassalle distinctly describes " Franz von Sickingen" as a drama " with a purpose," we have in it an explanation of the change that took place in his—still ideal—attitude towards the political tendencies of the time.

But it was not long before this change of attitude showed a leaning towards the views of the North German "Vulgar Demo- cracy," and that, too, with regard to a concrete question of the day.

" Franz von Sickingen " was finished in the winter of 1857-1858. Lassalle, as he writes to Marx, had already conceived and begun it while still working at the "Heraclitus." It had been, he says, a necessity to him to escape now and then from that abstract world

---

[1] A word of explanation as to this word " Kleindeutsch "—literally " Small German." I may remind my English readers that before the German Empire had been established, there were, amongst Germans, great differences of opinion as to the way in which the unification of Germany was to be brought about. One party—composed chiefly of Protestant middle - class persons in North Germany — was for uniting Germany under the supremacy of one of the two great rival German powers— *i.e.*, Prussia, thus excluding Austria. But as this also meant the ex- clusion of some seven million Austrian Germans, the party was dubbed " Kleindeutsch " by their opponents. Their opposition to Austria being largely based upon the Catholicism of Austria, they went in for a good deal of " no popery " agitation. They were, moreover, opposed not only by the Catholic party and Ultra Conservatives, but by all the Radical parties, who were in favour of one great German Commonwealth, embrac- ing all German peoples.

of thought, in which, during that work, he had had to "emmesh himself," and to turn to a subject which bore directly upon the great struggles of humanity. And so he had between whiles also studied the Middle-Ages and the Reformation period. He had "been drinking deep" of the works and life of Ulrich von Hutten, when the reading of a wretched "modern" drama, which had just appeared, suggested the idea: "THAT—the struggle of Hutten— would be a subject worth treating." And thus, without originally thinking of himself as the poet to carry out this design, he had sketched the plan of the drama. But soon it had become clear to him that he must also complete it himself. "A kind of inspiration" had possessed him. And, indeed, one feels that the drama was written with his warm heart's blood. Despite the faults I have pointed out, it, nevertheless, towers immeasurably above the whole democratic literature of the period. Not one of his German contemporary poets could have done better than Lassalle.

. . . . . .

I had just concluded this chapter when, owing to the kindness of Frederick Engels, the letters of Lassalle, found among Karl Marx' papers, were placed in my hands. Among these letters is an extremely interesting one addressed to Marx and Engels; it consists of 34 quarto pages, and refers exclusively, with the exception of a few lines, to "Franz von Sickingen." When the drama appeared in print Lassalle had sent three copies to Marx: one for himself, one for Engels, and one for Feiligrath, and had, at the same time, asked for their frank criticism of the play. Marx and Engels both acknowledged the many merits of the drama, and both independently—Marx was living in London, and Engels at this time was living in Manchester—seem to have come to much the same conclusions as to its faults. So much did their criticisms coincide that Lassalle replies—in the long letter just referred to— to both at once, because, as he says, "the letters without being absolutely identical, deal, on the whole, with the same points." And Lassalle's letter shows that these points were those which we have also urged above. "You both agree," writes Lassalle, "that even

Sickingen is drawn too much in the abstract." This says in a nut-shell what I have also enlarged upon. Lassalle's Sickingen is not the warrior knight of the early sixteenth century. He is the nine-teenth century Liberal, masquerading in the latter's armour, *i.e.*, liberal ideology. His speeches are for the most part altogether out of keeping with the period in which they are supposed to be spoken. "You both agree," writes Lassalle in another passage, "that I have too much left in the background the peasant move-ment,". . "that I have not given it sufficient prominence.". . " You [1] (Marx) found your argument upon this : I should have made Sickingen and Hutten perish, because they, like the Polish nobles, were only revolutionary in their own imagination, but in reality represented a *reactionary* cause. ' The aristocratic repre-sentatives of the Revolution,' you (Marx) say, ' behind whose catchword of unity and freedom there ever lurks the dream of the old empire and of " Faust recht,"[2] ought, therefore, not to absorb all the interest as they do with you, but rather the representatives of the peasants, and especially these and the revolutionary elements of the towns ought to have supplied a far more living background. Then, too, you could to a much greater extent have let the most modern ideas express themselves in their naïvest form, while now, as a matter of fact, besides religious freedom, bourgeois unity re-mains the main idea.' . . 'Have you not yourself,' you (Marx) exclaim, ' like your Franz von Sickingen, to some extent fallen in-to the diplomatic error of ranking the Lutheran-knightly op-position above the plebeian-burgher one ? ' " I have omitted Lassalle's intercalated remarks, because they mostly refer to other matter, and would here be unintelligible. In the main, Lassalle defends himself by trying to prove that he has given sufficient prominence to the knightly narrowness of Sickingen—so far as it really existed in the historical Sickingen—by this : that instead

[1] In writing to Marx, Lassalle, of course, always uses the familiar " du " —thou. Where he uses the plural form he is addressing both Marx and Engels.

[2] The practice of armed knights to waylay and plunder merchants travelling from town to town.

of appealing to the whole nation, instead of calling upon all the revolutionary forces in the empire to rise, and placing himself at their head, Sickingen begins, carries on his revolt as a knightly one, and he finally perishes because of the narrowness of his knightly means. And it is just in Sickingen's failing because he did not go far enough, that the tragic, and at the same time revolutionary, idea of the drama lies. Moreover, in the one scene of the play in which he brings the peasants themselves upon the scene, and in the frequent references to them in the speeches of Balthasar, etc., he had given them all the significance, and even more, than the peasant movement actually possessed. Historically, the peasant movement had been as reactionary as that of the nobles.

This latter view, as is well known, Lassalle also supported in several of his later writings, among others, in the " Workingmen's Programme." But, in my opinion, it is by no means a correct one. That the peasants formulated demands which meant a return to the past, does not, as such, stamp their movement as a reactionary one. Truly, the peasants were not a new class, but they were by no means like the knights, a decaying class. The reactionary part of their demands is only formal, not essential. This Lassalle overlooks, and as a Hegelian falls so completely into the error of deriving history from "ideas," that after Marx' remark, "Then, too, you could, in far greater extent, have let the most modern ideas express themselves in their naïvest form," he puts two marks of interrogation, strengthened by one of exclamation.

The rest of Lassalle's defence would be justified, if in the play there were even the slightest indication that Sickingen's confining himself to his knightly means was due to his own knightly limitations. But this is not the case. In the play, this is treated essentially as a *tactical* mistake. This suffices for the tragic idea of the drama, but does not set forth the historical anachronism of the Sickingen revolt, which was the actual cause of its failure.

CHAPTER III.

In the beginning of 1859, "Franz von Sickingen" appeared as a printed play. At the time of its publication Europe was on the eve of a war which was to react seriously upon the development of affairs in Germany. It was that Franco-Sardinian campaign, already agreed upon in the summer of 1858, at Plombières, between Louis Napoleon, and Cavour, for the freeing of Lombardy from Austrian rule, and the overthrowing of Austrian supremacy in central Italy.

Austria, at this time, belonged to the German Confederation, and so the question as to what attitude the rest of the Confederate States should assume in this contest was naturally raised. Was it the duty of the rest of Germany or not, especially as opposed to France, to identify itself with Austria?

The answer to the question was rendered the more difficult in that the nature of the war was an equivocal one. For the Italians concerned in it, it was a national war of emancipation, which was to help the cause of the unification and emancipation of Italy a step forward. For France, on the other hand, it was a cabinet war—a war undertaken to bolster up the Bonapartist *régime* in France, and to enhance the authority of France in Europe. This much, at any rate, was certain. Moreover, it was common talk that Napoleon had driven a pretty bargain with his ally, the King of Sardinia, that his support was to be paid for in territory (Nice and Savoy), and that the unification of Italy should, at that time, only proceed so far as was compatible with the interests of Bonapartist Imperialism. It was on these grounds that, *e.g.*, so impassioned an Italian patriot as Mazzini denounced, even at the end of 1858, the secret treaty concluded at Plombières between Napoleon and Cavour as a mere dynastic intrigue. This much,

44

at least, was certain, that whoever supported *this* war, was first of all supporting Napoleon III. and his plans.

But Napoleon III. needed support. Against Austria alone, he could, in league with Sardinia, wage war, but if the other states of the German Empire, and above all, if Prussia went to the aid of Austria, the affair became at once much more critical. And so, through his agents and his emissaries, he used every means at the German courts, in the German press, and with the German party leaders, to agitate against the war being treated as a matter that in any way concerned Germany. What possible interest could the German people have in upholding the despotism of Austria in Italy, or, indeed, in lending any support to so arch-reactionary a state as Austria? Austria was the sworn foe of the freedom of the peoples; if Austria were crushed, a fairer morning would dawn for Germany also.

On the other side, Austrian writers demonstrated that, if the Napoleonic plans in the South were realised, the Rhine would straightway be in danger. The next attack would be directed against it. Whoever wished to protect the left bank of the Rhine against the greedy hands of France, must assist Austria in maintaining her military position in northern Italy unhampered; the Rhine must be defended on the Po.

The watchword of the Napoleonic emissaries coincided in many essential points with the programme of the Kleindeutsch party (the unification of Germany under the leadership of Prussia, and the expulsion of Austria from the German Confederation), and was on exactly the same lines. Nevertheless, a large number of Kleindeutsch politicians could not make up their minds, just at this juncture, to separate the cause of Austria from that of the rest of Germany. This seemed to them the less admissible, since it was also known that Napoleon was carrying on the war in collusion with the Government of the Tzar at St. Petersburg; that this war, therefore, had the farther aim to aid and abet Russian intrigues in the south-east of Europe. They inclined far more to the opinion that the first thing to be done now was to repel Napoleon's attack. Only when this had been done could they discuss the matter further.   But until this was done the Italians, so long as they fought under the ægis of Napoleon, must put up with being treated simply as his confederates.

Now, it cannot be denied that, from the Kleindeutsch stand-point, another view of the situation might also have been arrived at, and that which has just been set forth deemed inconsequent. If Austria, and especially its extra-German possessions, were to be expelled—and that the sooner the better—from the German Confederation, why not gladly welcome an event which was a step towards the realising of this programme ?   Had not Napoleon declared he was fighting only Austria and not Germany ?   Why, then, support Austria against France, especially as doing this also entailed war against the Italians, who surely were fighting for the justest cause in the world ?   Why defend the Rhine before it was attacked, before there was even a hint that any attack was intended ?   Why not rather turn the difficulty of Austria and Napoleon's manœuvres in Italy to account in furthering the cause of the unification of Germany under the leadership of Prussia, and that by positive methods ?

To this—I repeat—from the Kleindeutsch standpoint, logical policy, Lassalle gives expression in his work published at the end of May, 1859: "Der Italienischer Krieg und die Aufgabe Preussens."[1] With great energy he combats the view advocated in the two Berlin organs of North German Liberalism, the *National Zeitung* and the *Volks Zeitung*—in the former, among others, by Lassalle's subsequent friend, Lothar Bucher—that, in face of an attack emanating from Bonaparte, Prussia, as a member of the Con-federacy, must stand by Austria.   Lassalle, on the contrary, demanded that Prussia should seize upon this moment to impress upon the Kleindeutsch states its German supremacy, and, if Napoleon reconstructed the map of Europe in the south on the principle of nationalities, to do the same, in the name of Germany, in the north ; and if he liberated Italy, Prussia on its side should seize Schleswig-Holstein.   The moment had now come, " while the decay of Austria was proceeding of itself, to provide for the raising

[1] " The Italian War and the Mission of Prussia."

of Prussia in the estimation of the Germans." And, he adds in conclusion, "the Government may be assured of this. In this war, which is of as vital interest to the German people as it is to Prussia, the German democracy itself would carry the standard of Prussia; would sweep all obstacles from its path with an expansive force of which only a seething outburst of national passion is capable; a passion which, crushed down for fifty years, stirs and palpitates in the heart of a great people."

On the strength of this pamphlet, attempts were subsequently made to stamp Lassalle as an advocate of the "German" policy of Bismarck, and it cannot be denied that the national programme set forth in it bears as such a great resemblance to that of the National Club founded in the summer of 1859, and, in the same way, *mutatis mutandis,* to the policy pursued by Bismarck in bringing about the unification of Germany under the leadership of Prussia. But then Lassalle, for all his theoretical radicalism, was still in practice pretty much imbued with Prussian jingoism. Not that he was a narrow Prussian "Particularist"—we shall soon see how far removed he was from that—but essentially he looked at the national movement, and its relations to foreign policy, through the spectacles of a Prussian democrat. In this respect his hatred of Austria was just as exaggerated as the Prussophobia of many South German democrats, and even many Socialists. For him Austria is "the most dangerous state-concept in regard to all culture that Europe can show;" he would "like to know the negro who, placed by the side of Austria, would not seem white;" Austria is "a reactionary principle;" "the most dangerous enemy of all ideas of freedom;" "the state-concept Austria must be crushed, destroyed, torn to shreds, annihilated—scattered to the four winds." Every political infamy with which Napoleon III. might be reproached, Austria also has upon its conscience. And, "if the reckoning were otherwise pretty equal, yet, despite his patronage of the priests, Louis Napoleon has *not* signed the Roman *Concordat.*" Even Russia fares better than Austria. "Russia is naturally an empire of barbaric force, which its despotic Government is trying to civilise

as far as is compatible with its despotic interests. Barbarism has
here the excuse that it is a national element."   It is altogether
otherwise with Austria.   " Here the Government, in opposition to
its peoples, represents a barbaric principle, and artificially and
violently crushes them beneath its yoke."

In this one-sided and relatively—*i.e.*, relatively if we compare
it with other states—exaggerated blackening of Austria, and also
in many other points, Lassalle's pamphlet is at one with a work
which had appeared a few weeks earlier, the drift of which was
also to exhort the Germans to leave Napoleon, so long as he
played the part of Liberator, a free hand in Italy, and to applaud
the annihilation of Austria.   This work was the notorious one of
Herr Karl Vogt : "Studien zur gegenwärtigen Lage Europa's,"[1] a
shameless piece of hack work, strung together in the Bonapartist
interest.   I should have hesitated to quote this work in connection
with Lassalle's, were Lassalle not so entirely above all suspicion
of complicity with Vogt and his crew, that it is impossible to
place him in a false light by a comparison, which on theoretical
grounds seems to me necessary, of these works.   But farther, I
shall now quote a passage from the preface to the " Herr Vogt "
of Karl Marx, the work which proved that Vogt was at this time
writing and agitating in the interest of Bonaparte, proofs which
were substantiated nine years later by documents found at the
Tuileries.   This passage fits in here because it indubitably refers
to Lassalle.   Marx writes : " Men who even before 1848 were in
accord that the independence of Poland, Hungary and Italy, was
not only a right of those nations, but was also in the interests of
Germany and of Europe, expressed altogether contradictory views
with regard to the policy to be pursued against Louis Bonaparte
by Germany on the occasion of the Italian war of 1859.   This
contradiction arose from contradictory views as to actual assumptions—to decide between which must be left to a later time.
I, for my part, have in this work only to do with the opinions of
Vogt and his clique.   Even the opinion which he *professed* to
represent, and in the imagination of a number of uncritical persons

[1] " Studies on the present situation in Europe."

did represent, does not, in point of fact, come within the scope of my criticism. I deal with the opinions which he *really* re-presented." [1]

In spite of this, it was naturally unavoidable that where Vogt used arguments which also occur in Lassalle, the latter is also criticised in Marx' work. This, however, did not prevent Lassalle from declaring in a letter to Marx, dated 19th January, 1861, that after reading " Herr Vogt," he thought Marx' con-viction that Vogt was bribed by Bonaparte, "perfectly right and justifiable," while the internal proof of this—that Vogt was a somewhat doubtful personage, Lassalle, who originally defended Vogt, had admitted earlier—was "supported by an immense weight of evidence." The book was " in *every* respect a masterly thing."

At any rate, " Herr Vogt " is an extremely instructive book for the understanding of the history of the nineteenth century. This pamphlet contains a mass of historical material that would suffice to furnish forth a dozen essays.

But from our point of view it has also a special interest.

The correspondence between Marx and Lassalle was at no time so active as in the years 1859 and 1860, and a large portion of it deals with this Italian war and the attitude to be taken in regard to it. Whether the letters of Marx to Lassalle on this subject are still in existence, and if so, in whose hands they are, is not at present known, nor whether their present owner is prepared to publish them.

From Lassalle's letters, however, the attitude taken by Marx at this time can only be imperfectly gathered, and still less the reasons for it, since Lassalle, quite naturally, confines himself chiefly to explaining his own standpoint, and refuting, as far as possible, the objections to it. But no further explanation is necessary to explain why, in a work on Lassalle, written for Socialists, not only his personal relations to the founders of modern scientific Socialism, but also his relation to their theoreti-cal teaching and their treatment of social and political questions are of especial interest.

---

[1] Karl Marx : " Herr Vogt." Preface, v. vi.

The *literati* of the day have, as we all know, a cut and dried formula as to this relation. As to politics, in the narrower sense, it runs thus : Lassalle was national ; Marx and Engels were and are international ; Lassalle was a German patriot ; Marx and Engels were and are without fatherland, they ever cared only for the Universal Republic and the Revolution ; what became of Germany was a matter of indifference to them.

I regret that there is a bitter disillusion in store for the inventors of this formula and those who repeat it.

Even before Lassalle's " *Italienischer Krieg* " (" Italian War ") appeared, the same publishers had issued another pamphlet, dealing with the same subject. It was entitled " *Po und Rhein* " (" The Po and the Rhine "). Like the first edition of Lassalle's work, it appeared anonymously. The author sought to prove, from the military point of view, that the watchword given by the organs of the Austrian Government, that Germany needed the Italian provinces for its defence in the south-west, was false ; that without these provinces Germany still had a strong defensive position in the Alps. This would be especially the case so soon as a free and united Italy had been created, since Italy would hardly be likely ever to have any valid reason for quarrelling with Germany, but might often enough have cause to seek a German alliance against France. Northern Italy was an appanage which at the very most might be useful to Germany in war, but could only be a danger in times of peace. And even the military advantage in a war would be bought at the price of the sworn enmity of 25 million Italians. But, the author then continued, the question of the possession of these provinces is one between Germany and Italy, and not between Austria and Louis Napoleon. Face to face with a third factor, a Napoleon, who interfered only to further his own, in other respects anti-German, interests, it was simply a question of a province that one only cedes under compulsion, of a military position one only evacuates when it is no longer tenable. " If we are attacked we shall defend ourselves." If Napoleon wanted to pose as the paladin of Italian Independence, let him begin at home, and restore Corsica to the Italians. Then it might be seen how far he was in earnest. But if the map of Europe is to be revised, "then we Germans have the right to demand that it shall be done thoroughly and impartially ; that it shall not be after the approved fashion of demanding that Germany alone should make sacrifices." "But the final result of this whole investigation," the pamphlet concludes, "is that we Germans would be driving an excellent bargain if we exchanged the Po, the Mincio, the Etsch, and the whole Italian bag of tricks for the UNITY of Germany . . . which alone can make us strong at home and abroad."

The writer of this pamphlet was no other than—Frederick Engels. Needless to say that Engels had published it in agreement with Karl Marx. Lassalle had found a publisher for it. And Lassalle had also, as appears from one of his letters, reviewed it in the Vienna *Free Press*, at that time still an independent organ, whose editor was a relative of his. So he was quite familiar with its contents when he wrote his " Italian War," and therefore opposes it when he combats its conclusion that, as Napoleon's leadership transformed the war from a war of independence into an enterprise directed against Germany, which must, of necessity, end in an attack upon the Rhine, Germans must treat it as such. On the other hand, as I have already said, Lassalle's work was also criticised in the criticism of " Herr Vogt," [1] in Part V. 14, " Dâ-dâ Vogt and his Studies."

[1] So, too, in a second pamphlet by Engels : " Savoyen, Nizza, und der Rhein " (" Savoy, Nice, and the Rhine "). Lassalle in his pamphlet had declared the annexation of Savoy to France a quite self-evident, and provided Germany received a satisfactory equivalent for this increase of territory, a " perfectly unobjectionable " proceeding. Now Engels showed what an extraordinarily strong military position the possession of Savoy would give to France, *vis-à-vis* of Italy and Switzerland, a matter which surely also deserved to be taken into consideration. Sardinia abandoned Savoy because, for the time being, it got something more in exchange. But the Swiss were by no means edified at the transaction. Their statesmen—Stämpfli, Frei-Herrosé, among others—did their utmost to prevent the delivering over into the French hands of the ground of Savoy, hitherto neutral. In " Herr Vogt " may be read an account of the manœuvres by which the Bonapartist agent in Switzerland counteracted these efforts. The rest may be seen by a mere glance at an atlas.

How strikingly Lassalle's arguments frequently coincided with those of Vogt one example will show. On the side of Austria the treaties of 1815 had been referred to, by which the possession of Lombardy had been guaranteed to Austria. To this Vogt and Lassalle reply as follows :—

Vogt.	*Lassalle.*
"It is remarkable to find such language in the mouth of *the only Government*" (the italics are Vogt's) "which has, so far, impudently violated the treaties. All other Governments have, so far, respected them ; Austria alone has violated them, by stretching out in the midst of peace, and without any provocation, its wanton hand against the Republic of Cracow, protected by these same treaties ; and, without more ado, incorporating it with the Austrian Empire." (" *Studien*," 1st Ed., p. 58.)	" The treaties of 1815 could no longer, even from the diplomatic point of view, be appealed to. Seriously violated by the creation of the Belgian Constitution, trodden under foot and torn to shreds by this same Austria, through the forcible occupation of Cracow, against which the Cabinets of Europe did not fail to protest, they have lost all righteous validity for every member of the European state family." (" *Italienischer Krieg*," 1st Ed., p. 18.)

Now, let us hear Marx against Vogt : "Nicolas, of course, destroyed the Constitution and Independence of the Kingdom of Poland, guaranteed by the Treaties of 1815, out of 'respect' for the Treaties of 1815. Russia respected the integrity of Cracow in no less degree when, in the year 1831, it invested the Free City with Muscovite troops. In the year 1836 Cracow was again invested by Russia, Austria, and Prussia ; was in all respects treated as a conquered country ; and even in the year 1840, on the strength of the Treaties of 1815, appealed in vain to England and to France. Finally, on the 22nd February, 1846, the Russians, Austrians, and Prussians once more invested Cracow, in order to hand it over to Austria. The treaty was violated by the THREE NORTHERN powers, and the Austrian Confiscation of 1846 was only the last word of the Russian entry of 1831." ("Herr Vogt," pp. 73, 74.) Further, in a note, Marx refers to his pamphlet, "Palmerston and Poland," in which he had shown that Palmerston, since 1831, had also had a hand in the intrigues against Cracow. This, however, is a question which has no special interest for us here, but it is of interest to note another matter demonstrated by Marx : that Vogt, in referring to the example of Cracow, was again only repeating and paraphrasing an argument advanced by the Bonapartists. In a Bonapartist pamphlet, published at Paris in the beginning of 1859, by Dentu : " La vraie question—France, Italie, Autriche " ("The real question—France, Italy, Austria ")—it was said literally : " Moreover, with what right could the Austrian Government appeal to the inviolability of the Treaties of 1815, that Government which violated them by the confiscation of Cracow, whose independence these treaties had guaranteed ? " After the true sycophant method, Vogt had everywhere played an extra trump. Such catch words as " the only Government," " in impudent fashion," " wanton hand," are his stock-in-trade. And so, too, when at the end of the passage quoted above he pathetically invokes a " political Nemesis against Austria."

Lassalle, when he wrote his pamphlet, had not yet seen Vogt's production ; but that his work was influenced by the " cries " set going by Bonaparte, and repeated through a thousand channels in the press at home and abroad, the above quotation, to which a whole series of others of the same kind might be added, leaves no doubt. When the National Liberal Bismarck worshippers to-day claim that the policy of their idol was sanctioned even by Lassalle, they are overlooking only one fact : that the programme proposed to the Prussian Government by Lassalle, in whatever sense Lassalle himself meant it, was to all intents and purposes the same as the programme which Bonaparte was then trying to palm off upon the German patriots, in order to win them over to his temporary policy. All the "prophecies " in the " Italienischer

Krieg," which to-day excite the admiration of the Brandeses, etc., are also to be found in Vogt's "Studien," and in a whole series of other Bonapartist pamphlets. Yes, Herr Vogt knew, even as early as 1859—*before* the re-organisation of the Prussian army—that should Prussia stir up a German civil war, for the re-establishment of a unified central power, this war " would not last as many weeks as the Italian campaign would months." [1] Moreover, Vogt, who was " in the swim," was really better informed on many points than Lassalle, a fact which should be distinctly noted to Lassalle's honour. Vogt, *e.g.*, knew perfectly that the Berlin Cabinet would leave Austria in the lurch. According to him, it must be clear even to the " most short-sighted person," that " an understanding existed between the Prussian Government and the Imperial Government of France, that Prussia would not draw the sword in defence of the extra-German Provinces of Austria . . . that Prussia would prevent any attempt of the Confederation or the individual members of the Confederation on behalf of Austria . . . in order to receive its wage for these efforts, in North German lowlands." [2] More predictions cannot really be expected from a prophet.

Lassalle, on the other hand, seems, just at this time, to have been very inadequately advised of the intentions of the Berlin Cabinet by his informants. "My pamphlet, '*Der Italienischer Krieg und die Aufgabe Preussens*'" ("The Italian War and the Mission of Prussia"), he writes, on the 27th May, to Marx and Engels, " will have reached you. I don't know if you over there read enough German papers to see from them, at least approximately, what the feeling here is. *Absolute* Franco-phobia, hatred of France (Napoleon only the pretext, the revolutionary development of France the real, secret reason), that is the string on which *all* the papers here are harping, and the passion which by playing upon the national sentiment they are trying—unhappily with some success—to instil into the heart of the lower classes and democratic circles. Useful as a war against France, undertaken by the Government *against* the will of the people,

---

[1] " *Studien*," 2nd Ed., p. 155.   [2] "*Studien*," p. 19.

would be for our revolutionary development, just so dangerous must be the effect upon our democratic development of a war supported by blind popular enthusiasm. And besides other reasons adduced under this head in the 6th chapter of my pamphlet there is this : that they are already allowing the rift that divides us from our Governments to be entirely and completely closed. In the face of so menacing a danger, I felt it my duty to throw myself into the breach. . . . Of course, I am not for a single moment deluding myself into a belief that the Government could or would take the way proposed under Section III. On the contrary ! But I felt all the more bound to make this *proposal*, because it at once turns to a reproach. It may act as a sea-wall, against which the waves of this false popularity are beginning to break."

From this it appears that Lassalle, in writing his pamphlet, was more anxious to forward the revolutionary than the national movement—to subordinate the latter to the former. The idea in itself was right enough. The only question was whether the means were right ; whether these must not force the national movement—as to which, for the time being, there was absolutely no difference of opinion between Lassalle on the one hand, and Marx and Engels on the other—into a wrong path. Marx and Engels were of opinion that the first thing to do was to counteract the manœuvres directed against Germany as a whole, by the common action of all Germans, and at a time when such a plot was brewing, not to support, even apparently, a policy which must lead to the dismemberment of Germany. The difference of opinion between them and Lassalle on this question was mainly due to the fact that whilst they regarded the question from its wider historical and international side, Lassalle was influenced rather by the immediate relation of Germany's internal politics. Hence, too, arose the contradiction that while he strongly marked off the difference between the people and the Government of France, he identified Austria with the house of Habsburg, and proclaimed the destruction of Austria, when surely only the destruction of the Habsburg *régime* was involved.

In one of his letters to the well-known and remarkable Economist Rodbertus, Lassalle quotes a passage from a letter written by Rodbertus to himself: "And I yet hope to see the time when the heritage of Turkey shall have fallen to Germany, and when German soldiers, or Workers' regiments, are established on the Bosphorus." And to this Lassalle says: "It moved me strangely when, in your last letter, I read these words. For how often have I—in vain—pleaded for this very view against my intimate friends, and had to put up with being called a dreamer by them for my pains! All the putting off of the Eastern question that has been taken up so many times since 1839, has, to me, always seemed reasonable and logical, only because it must be put off until its natural reversioner, the German Revolution, solves it. We seem to have come into the world as spiritual Siamese twins." [1]

How Germany was to enter into the Turkish heritage, after Austria had first been "annihilated," and Hungary and the Slav States torn from Austro-Germany,[2] is difficult to understand.

Another passage from Lassalle's letters to Rodbertus fits in here : "If there is one thing I have hated in my life, it is the Kleindeutsch Party. Everything Kleindeutsch is Gothaism and Gagerism,[3] and pure cowardice. A year and a half ago, I held a meeting here of my friends, when I formulated the matter thus : We must all will for a united Germany, *moins les dynasties.* I have never written a line in my life that could be counted to the good of the Kleindeutsch Party ; I consider it as the product of sheer dread of earnestness, war, revolution, the republic, and as a good slice of national treason."[4]

It is evident that if Lassalle had been in earnest over the National Programme as set forth by him in " The Italian War,"

---

[1] Letters of Ferdinand Lassalle to Carl Rodbertus-Jagetzow, edited by Ad. Wagner. Letter of the 8th May, 1863.

[2] "*Italienischer Krieg,*" p. 30.

[3] "Gothaism "—*i.e.* the Gotha Party ; the name given the Kleindeutsch Party. Gagern, the " Statesman " of the Kleindeutsch Party.

[4] Letter of the 2nd May, 1863.

it would have been impossible for him to have written the above lines, for that programme was most certainly a Kleindeutsch one. He was rather only using it as it seemed to him expedient for his much more advanced political aims, and for bringing about the Revolution which was to solve the national question in the "greater" German sense. In his letters, following that of the 27th May, 1859, to Marx and Engels, he expresses himself more and more explicitly in this sense. Space forbids my giving more than certain parts and short *résumés* of Lassalle's very lengthy letters.

About the 20th June, 1859 (Lassalle's letters are very often undated, so that the date has to be determined from the context), Lassalle writes to Marx : " Only in a *popular* war against France . . . do I see a misfortune. But in a war *unpopular* with the nation, immense benefit for the Revolution. . . . The work then divides itself thus : our Governments must make the war (and they will do this), and we must make it unpopular. . . . You,[1] over there, absent from here ten years, seem to have no idea how little dis-monarchied our people is. I also only understood it, to my sorrow, at Berlin . . . now, if in addition to this, the people were induced to believe that the Government was conducting the war as a *national* one, that it had risen to the height of a *national* act, you would see how complete the reconciliation would be, and how, especially in case of reverses, the bond of 'German fidelity' would bind the people to its Government. . . . The following, then, is evidently to our interest :

" 1. That the war be made. (This, as already said, our Government will look after itself.) All the information I get from a *reliable* source bears out that the Prince is on the point of declaring for Austria." (The "reliable" source to which Lassalle here refers seems to have mystified him badly.)

" 2. That it (the war) shall be mismanaged. This, too, our Governments will themselves look after, and this the more completely, the *less* the people are interested in the war.

" 3. That the people shall be convinced that the war has been

[1] The " you " here refers to both Marx and Engels.

undertaken in an anti-popular, in a dynastic, and counter-revolutionary sense, therefore against their interests. This only we can look after, and to look after that is therefore our duty."

Lassalle then goes into the question, what end could be served by "wishing to stir up a popular war amongst us against France?" But here also there are two considerations which he accepts as conclusive. (1) The reaction upon the prospects of the revolutionary parties at home and abroad; and (2) the reaction upon the relations of the German Democracy to the French and Italian Democracies. The interests of Germany as a nation he does not touch upon at all. To the reproach that he was recommending the same policy as Vogt, who was writing in the pay of France, he answers: "Would you reduce me on account of the bad company I keep *ad absurdum?* Then I might return you the compliment, for you have the misfortune to be of one mind, this time, with Venedey and Waldeck." Then he boasts that his pamphlet has had an "immense" effect; that the *Volks Zeitung* and the *National Zeitung* had sounded a retreat; the latter "in a series of six leading articles, having executed a complete face about." Strange that Lassalle should never have asked himself *why* these organs of the Kleindeutsch school allowed themselves to be so readily converted !

In a letter to Marx in the middle of July, 1859—after Villafranca—he says : "It goes without saying that between us it was not principles, but rather as you say, and as I have always understood it, 'the most expedient policy,' upon which we differed." And that there may be no doubt in what sense he means this, he adds the words: "*i.e.,* therefore, after all, the most expedient policy for the Revolution."

In the beginning of 1860, he writes to F. Engels : "Only to avoid misunderstandings, I must say that even *last* year, when I wrote my pamphlet, I heartily wished that Prussia should declare war against Napoleon. But I wished it only on *this* condition, that the *Government* should declare it, and that it should be as unpopular, and as much hated by the people as possible. Then, truly, it would have been a great boon. But then, the Democracy ought not to have written and made propaganda for this war. . . As to the *present* situation, we are probably quite agreed, and shall, no doubt, agree also as to the future."

In the same letter, Lassalle also refers to the scheme of military re-organisation which was just then being broached, and which, as is known, subsequently led to conflict between the Government and the Liberal bourgeoisie. The mobilisation of 1859 had convinced the Prussian Government how ill prepared the Prussian army still was, and that drastic changes were necessary to fit it for taking the field, either against France or Austria, with any chance of success. Whoever then was in earnest about "the German mission of Prussia," must also endorse the re-organisation of the army, or, at least, must objectively admit its justification. This, in fact, the Progressists at first did. Now let us hear Lassalle : "The Bill is shameful ! Dissolution—complete, only masked, of the *Landwehr*, as the last democratic relic of the times of 1810—creation of an immensely powerful weapon for Absolutism and the Squirearchy—that, in two words, is the evident meaning of the Bill. Never would Manteuffel have dared to propose such a thing ! Never would he have carried it through. Whoever lives in Berlin now, and doesn't die of Liberalism, will never die of vexation !" Finally, one more quotation from a letter of Lassalle's to Marx, written from Aachen on the 11th September, 1860. Marx, in a letter to Lassalle, had referred, among other things, to a circular note of Gortschakoff's, which had declared that if Prussia went to the help of Austria against France, Russia on its side would intervene on behalf of France— *i.e.*, would declare war upon Prussia and Austria. This note, Marx had explained, was a proof, first, that there had all along been a plot of which the freeing of Italy was only the pretext, the weakening of Germany the real object, and secondly, that it was a shameless interference of Russia in German affairs, which must not be endured. To this Lassalle now replied that he could not see any insult in the note, but even supposing it did contain one, it would after all only affect "the German Governments." "For, *diable !* what does the strong position of the Prince of Prussia matter to you or me? As all his tendencies and interests are directed *against* the tendencies and interests of the German people, it is much rather in the interest *of the German people*, if the Prince's position is externally as weak as possible." So one must rather rejoice at such humiliation, or, at the most, only use it against the Government in the same way that the French had done under Louis Philippe.

It would be difficult to express oneself more "treasonably" than in all this, and those who have hitherto held up Lassalle as the pattern of a good patriot in the National-liberal sense of the word, against the Social Democracy of to-day, will, after the publication of Lassalle's letters to Marx and Engels, simply find they have not a leg to stand on. The motives that influenced Lassalle in writing the "Italian War" were anything but an acknowledgment of the national mission of the Hohenzollerns. And far from it being the case—as most of the bourgeois biographers declare—that in Lassalle the party-man was sunk in the patriot, it would be truer, on the contrary, to say that the party-man, the republican revolutionist, forced the patriot into the background.

Undoubtedly, the question might with a certain appearance of plausibility be asked: "But if the standpoint which Lassalle works out in his letters to Marx is so essentially different from the one set forth in the pamphlet, who can prove that the former was really the one which Lassalle in his inmost heart accepted? Since in any case he must have concealed his true face once, may not this have been from Marx?" There are so many reasons against this assumption that it is hardly worth while considering it. The most important is, that the contradiction between the pamphlet and the letters, is, after all, only an apparent one. Where Lassalle says anything in the pamphlet which does not square with the ideas expressed in the letters, he always speaks hypothetically, with a big "If." And to this "If" he adds at the end: "But if not—THEN," and formulates his "THEN" thus: "Then this will only prove again and again, that Monarchy in Germany is no longer capable of a national act." As to the positive declarations of the pamphlet, these he maintains also in the letters. He was perfectly sincere in the main contention of the pamphlet, that the Democracy—by which he understood the whole of the decidedly opposition parties—must not sanction the war against France, because they would thereby identify themselves with the oppressors of Italy ; and he was also quite in earnest in his desire for the crushing of Austria. Up to this point the pamphlet, whether one agrees with the standpoint set forth in it or not, is thoroughly justifiable as a subjective expression of opinion. Not so with regard to the last chapter. Here Lassalle transgresses the limits that divide the politician fighting for his convictions, for definite principles, from the demagogue. The former will never recommend anything which he does not really wish to happen. Lassalle certainly qualifies his expressions, but in so ambiguous a way that the uninitiated reader cannot but believe that Lassalle ardently desired the Prussian Government to pursue the policy which he there suggests. The qualified form explains the contradiction to the letters to Marx, Engels, and Rodbertus, but by no means justifies the double dealing. The lawyer trick of recommending a course because one believes it will not be taken, is, after all, an altogether false method in politics, only calculated to mislead your own followers—as, indeed, happened subsequently in this case. The example which Lassalle cites for his own tactics is the most unfortunate one imaginable. The foreign policy of the Republican opposition in France under Louis Philippe, of the gentlemen of the *National,* subsequently smoothed the path for the murderer of the Republic, for Bonapartism. Just as the " Pure Republicans " had used the Napoleonic legend against Louis Philippe, Lassalle believed he could play off the legend of Frederick the Great against the Prussian Government of the time. But the Frederick tradition, so far, at any rate, as it was here concerned, had, by no means, been given up by the Prussian Government, and Lassalle was making propaganda not *against*, but *for* the dynastic policy of the Hohenzollerns.

How later, when Prussia felt itself militarily strong enough, the policy was energetically followed ; how it next led to a civil war between North and South Germany; how Austria was happily forced out of the German Confederation, and the unification of the German rump consolidated, we have seen. But the realisation of the programme set forth in the "Italian War" bears the same relation to the one Lassalle dreamed of as the camel does to the horse of Lessing's fable.

Whither has the Prussian solution of the national question led Germany? Setting aside the question of Alsace and Lorraine — the annexation of these provinces was an additional blunder—let us only consider the position of the German people face to face with Russia and Panslavism. The expulsion of Austria from the German Confederation has furthered the panslavistic propaganda to the highest degree. The Austrian Government is, to-day, forced to make the Slavs one concession after the other; and, consequently, the latter are making ever greater demands. Where they would formerly have been content with a recognition of their language and nationality, they to-day wish to rule and to *oppress*. At Prag, to-day a Tchech town, the Tchech fraternised with the French Jingoes and drank to a war against the German. The incorporation of the German portions of Austria with Germany, will, of course, come sooner or later, but it will be under ten times more disadvantageous circumstances than before the glorious expulsion of Austria from the German Confederation. To-day, the German Empire is obliged to look calmly on, while these districts are being made more and more Slav. For the Bismarckian method of unifying Germany has made Russia so strong, that the present German policy has the greatest interest in the maintenance of even *this* Austria. Half a loaf is better than no bread. And assuredly so long as Tsarism, with its panslavist aspirations, rules in Russia, so long the existence as a state even of the Austria of to-day has justification.

Lassalle, of course, wanted something quite other than the mere expulsion of Austria from the Empire. He wanted the destruction, the annihilation of Austria, whose German provinces were to form an integral part of the one and indivisible German Republic. So much the less, then, should he have drawn up a programme, the immediate consequences of which must be a civil war in Germany, a war of North Germany against South, for the South Germans in 1859 were distinctly on the side of Austria. Only Lassalle's strong tendency to sacrifice to his immediate object all considerations outside it, can explain this return to a diplomacy which he had only just denounced with the utmost severity in "Franz von Sickingen."

Then, too, in the writing of the pamphlet, there was in addition the passionate longing of Lassalle to take part in actual politics. This longing again and again finds expression in his letters. When Lassalle, at this time, refuses to entertain any matter on the ground of the scientific work he was still contemplating, it is with the reservation : If there is any *immediate* possibility of influencing the development of the Revolution, then he will give up science also. Thus on the 21st March, 1859, he had written to Engels :

"Rather, I suppose, I shall henceforth devote myself to the study of national economy, the philosophy of history—I mean history in the sense of social development—unless, indeed, as is to be devoutly hoped, practical movements begin at last to stop all more serious theoretical activity." "How gladly would I leave unwritten what I perhaps *know*, if instead we [the "we" is here used as referring to the party,] may succeed in doing a little of what we *might*."

And could Lassalle, six weeks after writing this, have gone over to the monarchical "Kleindeutsch" camp ? No. His policy was wrong, but his aim had remained the same : the Revolution for the one and indivisible German Republic. That is what is meant when he prefaces his work with a motto from Virgil : "Flectere si nequeo superos acheronta movebo." If I am unable to influence the gods—the *Government*, I will move Acheron—the *people*.

CHAPTER IV.

"THE SYSTEM OF ACQUIRED RIGHTS," AND OTHER MINOR WORKS.

(1860-1861.)

LASSALLE'S next work, after the "Italian War," was a contribution to a periodical, appearing in book form, and edited, during the summer of 1860, by the democratic writer, Ludwig Walesrode, under the title of "Democratic Studies." This was the essay, subsequently issued as a pamphlet: "Fichte's Politisches Vermächtniss und die neueste Gegenwart."[1] It may be considered as an epilogue to the earlier work, where Lassalle says openly what he had thought well to put earlier in a veiled form. The "Political Legacy" of Fichte, as Lassalle explains, quoting from a sketch on a political essay found among Fichte's papers, "is the unification of Germany, but as a *unified Republic*; otherwise, a united Germany would anyhow be impossible. Were Germany conquered by any one of the existing German States, that would not constitute national unity; but only the forcing upon the other German races the specific *Haus-geist* [2] of the conquering tribe, and their becoming Prussianised, Bavarianised, Austrianised!" . . . . "And inasmuch as that balancing which is still possible between their different idiosyncrasies would disappear, the German people would find themselves uprooted in their spiritual life also."

"The conquest of Germany, not in the special '*Haus-geist*,' but rather by the free absorption of that spirit into the national spirit and its aims, would assuredly be something very different! But it would be sheer madness to expect the idealism of such a decision from men,"—Lassalle is speaking of the German princes, and especially of the King of Prussia—"whose mental personality,

---

[1] "Fichte's Political Legacy and the Immediate Present."
    i.e., local spirit.

64

like that of all other men, is a definite product of the various
factors in their education, traditions, inclination, and history; as
mad as to expect it of any one of us, had his training and education been exclusively determined by the same factors."

These are the last of Lassalle's own comments in the essay.
The rest is taken up with quotations from Fichte, demonstrating
how and why the unity of Germany is only possible on the basis
of "complete personal freedom," and that for this very reason, the
Germans, "in the eternal plan of the Universe," are called upon
to represent a "true kingdom of right," a kingdom of "freedom,
founded upon the equality of all that bear the face of man."
And, Lassalle concludes, "Far be it from us to weaken the inimit-
able strength of these words by adding any of our own." Then,
addressing the editor: "And now, dear sir, if I have not been able
to comply literally with your request (*i e.,* to write an article on a
"burning question of the day"), yet I think *your* object has been
attained, and mine also."

Now, what was Lassalle's "object" in publishing this essay,
which is dated January, 1860? This also we learn from a letter
to Marx. On the 14th April, 1860, Lassalle writes to the latter
explaining why he had accepted Walesrode's invitation, although
his whole time was taken up with the completing of a great work.
To begin with, he had found Walesrode a very honest man, brave
and stout-hearted, as his meritorious pamphlet, "Politische
Todenschau,"[1] proved, and who deserved that one should do
something for him. But then Lassalle continues: "Finally, the
book might, after all, produce some salutary effect upon our
German Philistines, and if I had refused the invitation, it
would in any case have been addressed to one far less determined
than myself. Yes, unquestionably, to some one coquetting with
monarchical or some such democratism, or Kleindeutsch ideas,
while the invitation gave me an opportunity of once again uttering
a genuine republican war-cry, and thus, in the name of our party,
taking possession of the book, which, it seems to me, from its
contents, although I know no particulars as to these or the contri-

[1] "Political Post-Mortem."

butors, was hardly likely to spread our ideas or strengthen the influence of our party.

"So, willy-nilly, an article came to be written. I have asked for a special advance copy of it only that I might send it to you. (The book itself will not appear till the October season.) I am forwarding it with this letter; please read it, then send it on to Engels, and finally write me if you like it.

"I believe that amid all this disgusting Gothaist turmoil it will produce the vivifying effect, that beyond the mountains there are yet men ; *that a Republican Party still lives ;* the effect of a trumpet-blast."

The book, the completion of which was at this time occupying Lassalle, was the "System der Erworbenen Rechte."[1] It is odd, and yet to anyone who has attempted a great work, comprehensible enough, to hear Lassalle complain that the thing is dragging so, and that he has "already conceived an intense hatred of it." But this "damned work," as he calls it in another passage of the same letter, was not to be finished even in the three months he now gave himself as a limit.

In 1860, Lassalle was again seriously ill with an attack of that chronic disease[2] to which he had already referred in the Düsseldorf Assize Court Speech, and from which he continued periodically to suffer. "I have been, and still am, very ill," he begins a letter to Marx, that must have been written at the end of January, 1860. "I have again been ill, and *worse* than before," is the beginning of the letter quoted above. "Have I been overworking of late, or is too long neglect taking its revenge now?" he continues. "In short, it seems my health has ceased to be that indestructible rock upon which I could once build so confidently." To get thoroughly cured, Lassalle, in the summer of the same year, went to Aachen. There he made the acquaintance of a young Russian, Sophie Solutzew, who had accompanied her father—who was also taking the waters—to Aachen. This young lady so fascinated Lassalle that he there and then, at Aachen, made her an offer of marriage.

[1] "System of Acquired Rights."
[2] Probably syphilis.

This, after a few weeks' reflection, Mademoiselle Solutzew declined.

All that has so far been made known of this episode in the agitated life of Lassalle, is through the account of Mademoiselle Solutzew, now the wife of a landowner in South Russia, published in 1877 in the St. Petersburg review, " *The European Messenger.*" A German translation of these statements was published a year later by F. A. Brokhaus, at Leipzig, under the title of "A Love Episode in the Life of Ferdinand Lassalle."[1] Everything was perfectly correct. Sophie Solutzew says that Lassalle certainly made a deep impression upon her, and that for a time she thought she might love him. But she was always doubting, until she became certain that a love that doubts is not love—above all is not the kind of love which Lassalle, with his references to the struggles that the future would bring him, expected. Possibly the prospect of these struggles frightened the young lady more than she is willing to admit ; the confessions of a journal and of "memoirs" notoriously never speak the whole truth. On the other hand, that view of the affair which counts it almost a crime on the part of Mademoiselle Solutzew to have

---

[1] When these statements of Mademoiselle Solutzew first appeared there were some who doubted the genuineness of them and of the letters of Lassalle which they contained. A German fifth or sixth rate penny-a-liner set himself to prove their apocryphal nature, to prove indeed that they were forged by the Countess Hatzfeld for her own honour and glory. But to anyone who knew the styles of Lassalle and Countess Hatzfeld, it is certain that even if the Countess had been foolish enough to plan the letters, she could never have been clever enough to write them. Further, in a legal action brought by Mademoiselle Solutzew, the genuineness of the letters was proved in court. I should not have mentioned this absurd *canard* except for the fact that the pamphlet of Kutschbach (the above-mentioned journalist) has induced an English writer of the position of Mr. Clement Shorter, to repeat this ridiculous story in his Preface to the new edition of Meredith's "Tragic Comedians." The "Lassalle Legend" has given rise to many silly statements, but to none more silly than the one that Lassalle's last love affair was also his first. It is true the love affair with Sophie von Solutzew was not particularly interesting.

been loved by Lassalle without returning his love, seems to me really a little too sentimental. The lady had a most unquestion- able right not to bestow her heart upon Lassalle, and Lassalle himself, passionate as his wooing was, very soon consoled himself for his mishap. Far more interesting than the love affair itself are the letters to which it gave rise from Lassalle to Mademoiselle Solutzew, above all the letter already referred to—"The Con- fession of a Soul," a MS. covering over thirty-five pages of printed matter. This is one of the most interesting documents for the understanding of Lassalle. If his first "journal" shows us the boy developing into a youth, here we see the youth grown into a man, and laying bare his inmost self. Surely what has just been said of "confessions" in general may apply also to this particular case, but one of the most remarkable characteristics of Lassalle is his—I might almost say, unconscious—sincerity. Lassalle's was, as his constant tendency to drop into the pathetic proves, a theatrically-inclined nature. He liked a little acting, and was far too much a society man to see any harm in using speech, according to Talleyrand's saying, to conceal his thoughts. And yet, as a human being he could not show himself other than he really was. His inclinations and his passions were far too strong not to betray themselves everywhere; his personality far too marked to hide itself under any disguise he might care to assume. Thus, even from the picture of himself which Lassalle drew for Sophie Solutzew, a picture in which he painted himself as he wished to appear to the young girl, the real Lassalle looks out—the real Lassalle with all his qualities and with all his defects.

In every line of this his huge self-confidence and vanity reveal themselves. I have said how in this MS. Lassalle suns himself in the light of his future fame; how he represents himself as the leader of a party, while, in fact, no such party as yet existed; depicts aristocracy and bourgeoisie as hating and fearing him, while at this time any cause for fear and hatred was wanting. In the same way he exaggerates his successes so far achieved. " Nothing, Sophie," he writes of the success of the Casket Speech, "can give you any idea of the electrical effect that I produced. The whole town, the population of the whole province, was, so to say, swimming upon the waves of enthusiasm . . . . all classes, the whole bourgeoisie, were drunk with enthusiasm . . . . this day secures me, in the Rhenish Provinces, the reputation of a transcendent orator, and of a man of unbounded energy, and the newspapers are spreading this fame through the whole kingdom . . . . since this day the Democratic Party in the Rhenish Provinces has recognised me as its chief leader." Then he writes of the Düsseldorf Trial that he came out of it " with not less glory." " I will give you my speech at this trial, as it also is published ; it will amuse you." He does not add that the speech was never delivered.

But along with the traits of perfectly child-like and childish vanity, there are not wanting those of legitimate pride ; legitimate, because founded upon principle and not upon any outward honours, while all through the letter rings a note of true conviction. Even when speaking of the "glory," which, with the occurrence of "certain events"—the expected revolution—would be shed upon the life of his future wife, Lassalle immediately adds : "But—is it not so, Sophie ?—that in such great matters, which make up the end and aim of the efforts of the whole human race, we must not merely speculate on individual happiness ;" and goes on, " and that is why we must in no wise reckon upon that."

In another respect, also, Lassalle's " Confession of a Soul " is of interest. In it he speaks very circumstantially of his relations to the Countess Hatzfeld. Now, though much in respect to his earlier relations to her may be idealised, this much, at any rate, is certain, that Lassalle could have no reason, when writing to a girl whom he was seeking in marriage, and whom he was trying so desperately hard to win for wife, to paint his feelings towards the Countess—beyond those of mere respect and gratitude—as being stronger than they really were. As a matter of fact, however, Lassalle in the letter indulges in expressions of positively passionate tenderness for the Countess. He loves her " with the tenderest filial love that has ever existed;" "three times as much as his own tenderly-loved mother." He demands of Sophie that if she accepts him for her husband, she shall "love the Countess with the true tenderness of a daughter," and hopes, although the Countess, being of "exceptional delicacy of feeling," and not knowing if Sophie Solutzew loves her, would not wish to live with the young couple, that they may be able to persuade her to, so that "all three may live happy and united."

From this it is evident that those who represent the Countess Hatzfeld during this time at Berlin, and later on also, as forcing herself upon Lassalle, have, to say the least, exaggerated enormously. The Countess Hatzfeld had her great faults, and, in my opinion, her friendship was, in many ways, extremely harmful to Lassalle; but because I think this, I feel it my duty to protest when this woman is unjustly dealt by. There could be nothing more ridiculous than the statement, made by several writers, and taken from the well-known pamphlet of Becker, that Lassalle had, later on, plunged into the Dönniges affair in order to get rid of the Countess.

Sophie Solutzew, moreover, speaks very favourably of the impression made upon her personally by the Countess Hatzfeld.

Three letters from Lassalle to Marx belong to this period of his stay at Aachen. Of course he in none of them refers to the Solutzew love affair. Only a few remarks, in one of the letters, as to the situation at the Russian Court, seem to point to the Solutzews as their source. But the letters contain much else that is interesting, and a passage in one of them is especially noteworthy, as it shows us what Lassalle, even at a time when he was on the best of terms with the Liberal Opposition leaders at Berlin, thought of the Liberal press, and of Prussian justice, which the Liberals were then praising to the skies. As it is as brief as drastic it may be quoted here.

Marx had tried to bring the editor of the Berlin *National Zeitung*, Zabel, to book for libelling him; Zabel having, under cover of Vogt's pamphlet, imputed the most dishonourable conduct to Marx. But before the case could come into court, Marx had been non-suited in three different courts. For the said justices of the *Stadtgericht*, the *Kammergericht*, and the *Ober Tribunal* of Berlin, all found that if Zabel repeated, and even trumped, all Vogt's calumnies against Marx, he could not possibly have had the intention to insult Marx. Such a proceeding as this Marx had, however, thought impossible even in Prussia, and wrote as much to Lassalle. To this Lassalle, who, from the beginning, had advised Marx against the action because justice was not to be hoped for anyhow, now replied as follows :—

" You write that you *now* know, that with us it depends upon the judges whether an individual can even get so far as to bring an action ! Dear fellow, how I wronged you once lately when in one of my letters I said you saw things in too dark colours ! I beat my breast remorsefully, and retract this entirely. Prussian justice, at any rate, you seem to have regarded in far too rosy a light ! But I've had to endure far other things than you from this crew ; could bring far stronger proof for what you say, have experienced far worse cases altogether at their hands, and that three times three dozen times, and in criminal, and more especially in purely civil cases. . . . Uff ! I must drive away the remembrance of all this. For when I think of this daily judicial murder of ten long years that I passed through, then waves of blood seem to tremble before my eyes, and it seems to me as if a sea of blood would choke me ! Well, I have got the better of all this long ago, and lived it all down, and time enough has expired since then for me to think of it all coolly. But never do my lips curl with so deep a smile of contempt as when I hear our judges and justice spoken of. Galley-slaves seem to me very honourable persons compared with our judges.

" But you will be quits with them, you write. ' At any rate,' you say, ' the Prussians provided you with material, the pleasant consequences of which they shall soon see in the London press ! ' No, dear friend, they will see nothing at all. Of course, I don't doubt that you will expose and annihilate them in the London press. But they will see *nothing* of this, *absolutely nothing ;* it will be as if you had not written at all. For English papers are not read by us, and you see, of our German papers not *a single one* will take any notice of it, not a single one will say even one poor little word about it. They'll take good care not to! And our Liberal press most of all! Where then would these calves-heads breathe the slightest word against their most sacred bulwark, ' the Prussian judges,' at the bare mention of which they gasp with admiration—why, they never utter the word but with inflated cheeks —and bow their heads to the ground with respect! Oh! nothing at all will they say of it, and from the Danube to the Rhine, and as far as ever 'the German tongue is spoken,' they will quietly ignore it in a conspiracy of silence. What's to be done against this press conspiracy? Oh! one may say what one likes, but our police is, after all, a far more liberal institution than our press! That—heaven help us! I really can find no other word for it—that is a mere ——." (The word Lassalle uses here is too strong to be reproduced in print : the reader may fill it in for himself.)

In 1861, Lassalle published, in the second volume of the "Demoscratische Studien," a short essay on Lessing, which he had written in 1858, on the appearance of Stahr's "Lessing's Leben und Werke."[1] Finally, in the same year he brought out his great work on the "Philosophy of Jurisprudence"—" Das System der Erworbenen Rechte " (" The System of Acquired Rights ").

The essay on Lessing is comparatively unimportant. Its form is still predominantly in the old Hegelian manner, and its matter inclines strongly towards the views set forth by Heine in his "Über Deutschland," with regard to Lessing's import for the literature and public life of Germany. Like Heine, Lassalle also extols Lessing as the second Luther of Germany; and when, at the end of the essay, referring to the great resemblance between the situation in Germany at that day, and the time of Lessing, he exclaims : " Like situations bring forth like characters," he may have been thinking of Heine's words : " Yes, a third man, too, will come, and he will conclude what Luther began, what Lessing continued, a man of whom the German fatherland stands

---

[1] " Life and works of Lessing."

in such sore need—the third liberator." For was it not Lassalle's
highest aspiration himself to become this third liberator? As in
the Hutten of his " Franz von Sickingen," as in the Lessing of this
essay, Lassalle's own attitude of mind is mirrored. Even the
apotheosis of the sword is not wanting. " But even when we have
carried out Lessing's conception in the domains of art, of religion,
and of history, how about politics?" asks Lassalle. And to remove
any possible doubts from the minds of those whom Lessing's
attitude with regard to the above-mentioned subjects had not yet
convinced, he quotes from Lessing's fragment " Spartacus." The
passage quoted is that where Spartacus, replying to the jeering
question of the consul : " I hear thou dost philosophize, Spartacus?"—makes answer :—" What? thou would'st not have me
philosophize. Philosophize! it makes me laugh! Well, then,
we will fight !"

Twenty years later this prophecy of Lessing's was fulfilled in the
French Revolution. And this solution would, according to Stahr,
"be also the end of the business between the Spartacus and the
consul of the future."

The "System of Acquired Rights" is Lassalle's chief theoretical
work. Although it is primarily written only for jurists, the subject with which it deals is far more akin to the practical struggles
of the present day than is that of the " Heraclitus." Hence I
shall attempt to explain, at least, the chief ideas of this work,
which Lassalle was justified in referring to on one occasion as " a
gigantic piece of human industry." On one point the specialists
are pretty well agreed—that " The System of Acquired Rights "
testifies at once to the extraordinary mental creative powers, as
well as to the juridical acumen of its author. On all these grounds
I shall be justified in dealing with this work at some length.

The task which Lassalle had set himself in writing this book,
which he divided into two parts, is shown by the sub-title : " Eine
Versöhnung des Positiven Rechts und der Rechts Philosophie."[1]
From the preface, which treats of the work of the Hegelian School

[1] " A Reconcilement of Positive Rights with the Philosophy of Jurisprudence."

in the domain of the law, it is at once seen to what an extent
Lassalle still relies on Hegelian principles. It is true he here
adopts an attitude more independent of Hegel than he had done
in the " Heraclitus," but he still holds not merely to the method,
but to the fundamental principles of the Hegelian philosophy—
i.e., not merely to the dialectic treatment of the subject to be in-
vestigated, and to the dialectic form of that investigation, but
also to the Hegelian idealism, to the tracing back of historical
phenomena to the development and the movement of ideas.
Like Hegel, Lassalle, too, stops half-way. He quite rightly points
out that the institutions of the law are not the realisations of
logically eternal, but of historical categories ; yet he deals with
these categories as with " realisations of mental concepts historically evolved," while he entirely ignores the question as to the
circumstances under which these mental concepts have developed,
as to the economic conditions whose expression they are. In fact,
he actually reverses that relation, and " tries to prove from the
concrete materials themselves, that the alleged purely positive and
historic facts are only the necessary outcome of the historical,
mental concept of the corresponding time." (Vol. I., p. 61.)[1]

Thus, despite the most brilliant display of acumen, Lassalle is
of necessity driven to erroneous conclusions.

As the most colossal example by which this causal dependence
of the so-called " purely positive and historic facts " upon historical
mental concepts, is demonstrated in his book, Lassalle refers to
his general exposition of the law of inheritance in the second
volume of his work entitled : " Das Wesen des Römischen und
Germanischen Erbrechts in historisch-philosophischer Entwick-
lung," (" The Nature of the Roman and Germanic Law of Suc-
cession in its Historical and Philosophical Development)." The
strength of this work lies in its unity, in its logical working out
of the main idea, and in its often really brilliant style. Through
all forms of law bearing upon the subject, Lassalle aims at working
out the Idea that the Roman law of inheritance is based upon the
Idea of the immortality of the subjective Will of the testator in

---

[1] The quotations are all from the Second Ed. of the " System,"

the heir, while in the old Germanic law of inheritance, the law
of intestacy (*i.e.*, of inheritance without testament) is mainly
based upon the idea of the family. This law is, therefore, exactly
what the Roman law is erroneously supposed to be, "the real
family law." This is right enough on the whole so far as it
goes. But now comes the weak side of Lassalle's work. His
dialectic, acute as it is, remains on the surface. It is true that
he again and again probes that surface, leaves no inch of it unex-
plored; but that which lies beneath remains absolutely untouched.
Why is it that the Roman law of inheritance expresses the continuity of the subjective Will? Because of the Roman concept of
immortality, because of the cult of the Lares and Manes. Why
is it that the Germanic law of inheritance is the family law?
"Because of the concept of the Germanic family." What is the
Roman concept of immortality? The continuity of the subjective Will. What is the concept of the Germanic family? "The
moral identity of those individuals who have for actual basis . . .
conscious unity of the mind or love." (Page 480.) This leaves
us exactly where we were. We are moving in a circle of ideas
and concepts, but get no explanation why these ideas here and
those concepts there were able to play the part assigned them.
Nor does Lassalle by a single word attempt to explain the juridical
notions and actual laws of the Romans and Germans by their
actual life conditions : the original source of the law everywhere appears as the *Volks-geist*.[1] And here Lassalle falls
into the same error with which he, quite rightly, elsewhere reproached former jurists. He certainly distinguishes between the
Roman and the Germanic *Volks-geist*, but he ignores the whole
of the historical development of the Roman people themselves.
He constructs, once for all, a Roman *Volks-geist* that embraces
all the thousands of years from the foundation of Rome to the
destruction of the Roman Empire—a "spirit" that stands in
about the same relation to the Germanic *Volks-geist*,—con-
structed after the same fashion—as does "Will to Love." (II. p.480,
note 3.) Of course, we must bear in mind that at the time

[1] " Folk-Spirit," *i.e.* " National Spirit."

when Lassalle wrote his "System of Acquired Rights," true historical research, with regard to the origin and development of Roman society, and of primitive Germanic society, was still in an elementary condition, and that even professed historians were still, on these matters, feeling their way in the dark. He can, therefore, not so much be reproached with not having answered the question correctly, as with not putting it correctly.

Indeed, a correct answer would not, at this time, have been possible. It is only through Morgan's epoch-making investigations that sufficient light has been thrown upon the primitive development of the different peoples, to allow us to understand why the Romans appeared in history with an entirely different law of inheritance from that of the Germanic races at the time of Tacitus. These were just then passing through the stage of development from the middle to the upper stage of barbarism; the transition from the matriarchate to the patriarchate, from syndyasmic marriage to monogamy, was not yet complete, they still lived in gentile groups founded upon consanguinity, and primitive communism yet prevailed. A law of inheritance based upon the subjective Will was, therefore, simply a matter of impossibility. If "Love"—a much more modern invention—has nothing, consanguinity has everything to do with the old Germanic law of inheritance. With the Romans, on the contrary, even before the abolition of the so-called kinship, the old order of Society, based upon personal blood-relationship, had begun to dissolve, and a new one, an actual state system, based upon territorial divisions and differences of property, been put in its place.[1] Private property in the soil, and the disruption of consanguineous groups as the economic unit, is the ground upon which the Roman Testament grew, not as a peculiar product of the Roman *Volks-geist*, but rather as a product of the same causes that created this special Roman *Volks-geist*, *i.e.*, the spirit that animated Rome at the time of the Twelve Tables.[2] If the Romans did give

[1] See F, Engels' "Ursprung der Familie, des Privat Eigenthums und des Staats. Im Anschluss von Lewis H. Morgan's Untersuchungen." 1st Ed., p. 93.   [2] About 450 B.C.

to the Testament a certain solemn consecration, this by no means justifies us in representing the Testament as a rite whose symbolised action—the transference of the Will—whose main point and substantial essence—the transference of property —were mere insignificant details. In certain stages of culture, even well into a state of civilisation, the people clothe all important economic acts in the form of religious rites ; we need but recall to mind the solemn rites at the partitioning of land, at the consecration of the marking of boundaries, etc. What would be thought of the historian who should represent the Roman Terminus-worship as a product of the peculiar nature of the Roman *Volks-geist*, the expression of a specially Roman " Idea," of which the main point was the concept of finiteness, and the bounding of the land only a secondary consideration ? What would be thought of a jurist who should ascribe the growth of Roman private property in land to the worship of the god Terminus ? Yet this is exactly what Lassalle does when he ascribes to the worship of the Manes and Lares, the origin of the growth of the Testament among the Romans, and traces its final cause to Roman mythology.[1]

In this way Lassalle arrives at a conclusion as unhistorical as it is illogical. He maintains that the Roman Law of the Twelve Tables, by assigning the heritage to which there was no testamentary heir, to the nearest agnate (*i.e.*, nearest of kin on the male side), and in the event of there being no agnate, to the Gens, proved that the Testament, in point of historical time, also appeared first, while the law of intestate inheritance was merely a subsequent and subsidiary introduction. As a matter of fact, it is this very Law of the Twelve Tables which, although it reverses the order of events, demonstrates the true course of historical development. It begins by enunciating the newly-introduced legal principle of testamentary freedom—that any one to whom the testator devises his property by testament shall be heir. But should there be no testament, the earlier law of inheritance again

---

[1] Recent researches have proved that ancestor-worship coincides amongst all people with the transition from the matriarchate to the patriarchate.

comes into force, the original law of intestacy; the heir is the nearest agnate, and then the Gens, *i.e.*, the primitive consanguineous group. The first institution historically appears last in the Twelve Tables, because, being the oldest, it is the most comprehensive, and as such naturally forms the final court of appeal. How essentially artificial, on the other hand, Lassalle's construction is, we may see from the fact that in order to maintain his theory that the Roman law of inheritance was based upon the "Concept of the Will," he is driven on one occasion to assert that " *absolutely no physical idea lies at the basis of the blood-relationship of the Agnates*" (Vol. II., p. 339), and to speak of the agnates as a "community of individuals brought about by the bond of force." (Vol. II., 323.) As orthodox old Hegelians, the ancient Romans have, " with cogent consistency of conception," arrived at the " profound proposition of speculative logic " that the unexpressed Will of the individual is the universal Will, whose content is " the universal Will of the people or the State in whose organisation the former is realised." (II., 323.) The testament and the freedom of testacy are older than the Roman State, but intestacy was introduced by the State. One fine day the State appointed agnates and the gentile community as subsidiary heirs, and this, not on the ground of an identical descent, but in its capacity of the State as by law established, as expressions of a common Will.

To-day, we know that the exact opposite was the case ; that it is not the State which conferred upon the Gens rights not formerly possessed by it, but rather that the State deprived the Gens of one right, and of one office after the other, constantly curtailed its functions, and that it was only with the disintegration of the gentile community, and with its internal dissolution, that the State, and with and through the State, the freedom of the testator, became possible.

As Lassalle knew nothing about the Gens, he, like all the jurists who at his time, and before him, dealt with the original Roman law of inheritance, was of necessity forced to arrive at false conclusions. But instead of coming nearer the truth than his predecessors, he seems rather to be further from it than they were. Bent upon constructing things out of the speculative concept, he cuts himself off from the possibility of recognising their actual connection. The celebrated Professor of Jurisprudence, Edward Gans—also a Hegelian—had represented the Roman laws of intestacy and of inheritance by testament as two antagonistic ideas, with no sort of common intellectual origin, and had endeavoured to explain them as a *historical* class difference between the Patricians and Plebeians. Erroneous as this interpretation is, the idea underlying it is right, *i.e.*, that we here have to do with a fundamental antagonism, and that the two opposing concepts of law sprang up upon different historical soils. Lassalle, however, in this very interpretation, discovered a relapse into the "error of the historical school," which assumes that "what should be deduced from the Idea" is "an external and historical event." (Vol. II., p. 318.) And, on the other hand, Lassalle declares it is a "fundamental error," when the other jurists start from the assumption that "the Roman law of intestacy is, in its Idea, a true family law." As a matter of fact, it is nothing else. Only that the family here considered does not coincide merely with the Roman family, but comprehended the wider gentile group.[1]

We cannot here enter more fully into this question, but even from what has already been said, we may see that the edifice so ingeniously raised by Lassalle rested upon an absolutely untenable foundation. Close and severely logical as the argument is, dexterous and witty as the analysis is, shrewd as many of Lassalle's

---

[1] The Romans, too, use the word *familia* not simply to denote the individual family, gathered into one house under one head, but also for the more or less loose union of the gentile group. A passage from Ulpian, quoted by Lassalle, explicitly distinguishes between the "familia" in the narrower sense *(jure proprio)* and the "familia" in the wider sense *(communi jure)*. To the latter "all those belong . . . who have sprung from the same family and the same gentile group." (See "System," etc., II., p. 343.) To Lassalle the above passage is a further proof that the Roman law of intestacy was *not* a family inheritance. "For," says he, among other things, "surely no one would represent the laws of inheritance of the gentile group as a family law of inheritance."

commentaries are, that which he meant the whole of his book to demonstrate with regard to the Roman law of inheritance he has not demonstrated. The Roman Idea of immortality is not the basis of the Roman Testament, but its ideological garment: it explains its form, but not its content. This still remains even when the religious background disappears. And to my thinking, the many forms and formalities upon which the Romans made the validity of Testaments contingent, were but a further proof that the Testament was not, as Lassalle thinks, the earlier, but on the contrary the later institution, and that probably—as with the Germans also, after they had adopted the Roman law—it was, for a long time, the exception, while intestate inheritance was still the rule.

But what is the practical application which Lassalle draws from his theory that the Testament is only to be explained by the Roman Idea of immortality—*i.e.*, the perpetuation of the subjectivity of the Will after death—and that with this explanation it must "as a concept" stand or fall? That after the Roman immortality of the Will had yielded to the Christian Idea of the immortality of the Spirit, an immortality no longer based upon the external world, but upon the "Spirit withdrawn into itself," the modern law of Testament was nothing more than a huge mistake, a "compact theoretical impossibility?" (II., 494.) This brings us to the first part of his work, of which the second, despite its being complete in itself, is, after all, only a kind of appendix.

The first part of the "System der Erworbenen Rechte" bears the sub-title : "Die Theorie der Erworbenen Rechte, und der Kollision der Gesetze."[1] In it Lassalle endeavours to establish a legal and scientific principle which shall once for all determine under what circumstances, and how far laws may be retroactive without violating the idea of right itself. In other words, where a new law or right comes into collision with an old law or right, when the former and when the latter is to be final ; when a right is to be respected really as an "acquired" right, when it is to be made retroactive without any further ado.

In answering this question, the weakness of Lassalle's method

[1] "The Theory of Acquired Rights, and the Conflict of Laws."

of investigation mentioned above is less noticeable, while all its advantages, the acuteness of perceptive thought, the comprehension —within certain limits—of the historic moment, together with a revolutionary audacity in following out an idea to its ultimate consequences, stand out conspicuously. And thus the result is far more satisfactory than in his inquiry into the nature of Roman Law. At whatever value we may estimate such inquiries into legal-philosophic themes, it certainly cannot be denied that Lassalle solves the question stated above in such a way that both jurist and revolutionist comes by his own. And that is surely no inconsiderable performance. Lassalle begins by laying down the two following propositions as premisses :

" (a) No law should be retroactive which affects an individual only through the medium of the action of his will.

" (b) Every law should be retroactive which affects the individual without the interposition of such a voluntary act ; which therefore affects the individual directly in those qualities of his which are involuntary, whether human or natural qualities, or socially acquired qualities, or which affects him only by altering the organic institutions of Society itself."

A law, *e.g.*, which alters the private rights or the civic prerogatives of the inhabitants of a country, comes into force at once. But such a law leaves untouched the acts of an individual taken by him on the ground of hitherto existing privileges, even though these privileges are themselves cancelled by the law. If to-day a law raises the age of legal majority from 21 to 25, all persons over 21 and under 25 are deprived of the rights pertaining to persons of full legal age, which they had hitherto possessed, for they did not possess these rights by any individual act of the will. But the new law would not be retroactive with regard to any legal business executed before the passing of the law, on the strength of their hitherto acknowledged legal coming of age. Only a right obtained through individual doing and willing, through the special action of the will of individuals, is an acquired right.

But even a right acquired by an individual act of the will is not, under all circumstances, exempt from the retroactive effect.

"The individual can only secure for himself, and for others, rights in so far, and for so long, as the laws always existing recognise the essence of these rights as a legitimate one." (I., p. 163.) "To every contract the clause should be tacitly added at the outset that the right therein stipulated for, either for himself or others, shall only hold good so long as legislation shall recognise such right as generally permissible." (I., p. 164.) "The only source of right," Lassalle explains, "is the common consciousness of the whole of the people, the universal *Geist* (Spirit)." By acquiring a right, therefore, the individual could "never wish to exempt himself from the working of the universal sense of right. Only such an individual could really be exempt from this working who, were such a thing conceivable, neither *now nor at any time, wished to acquire, to exercise, or to possess any right.*" (I., p. 165.) "No individual can drive a stake into the soil of law by means of which he should claim sovereignty for all time and in despite of any future, compulsory, and prohibitive legislation." (I., p. 166.) It is only "this desired self sovereignty of the individual that lies at the bottom of the claim that an acquired right shall still hold good even when prohibitive laws have rendered it invalid." If, therefore, public opinion has developed to the point of demanding henceforth the abrogation of some former right, *e.g.*, villenage, serfdom, the corvée, and socage ; forced services and tributes of a special kind, hunting rights, exemption from land taxes, entail, etc., there could in such case "be absolutely no question " . . . . of "any kind of infringement of acquired rights." Thus, the decrees of the celebrated night of the 4th August, 1789, by which the French National Assembly abolished all privileges based upon feudal supremacy, "violated no right and did not imply any retroactive effect." In this case there was nothing to "give compensation for." To admit a right to compensation, Lassalle pertinently says, even where the content of the right is abolished, had already been so prohibited by the public conscience, *i.e.*, had been declared contrary to right, would, "logically followed out, mean nothing less than the investing of classes or individuals with the right to levy a tax upon the public conscience for progressing." There can only be a question of compensation where not the principle of right itself, but only certain forms of exercising it are abolished, where not a particular class of legal objects, but only single examples of the same, were removed from the sphere of private to that of public law. It was upon this principle, Lassalle shows, that the French Assemblies after 1789 invariably proceeded " with true logic." On the other hand, the Prussian law of March 2, 1850, for example, on the commutation of the feudal dues of the peasants, was, in a large number of its provisions, nothing but a violation of the property—'contrary to right, and contrary to the sense of right'—of the poorest classes for the benefit of the noble landowners, *i.e.*, 'logically followed out,' nothing but a robbery."[1]

---

[1] Lassalle also speaks strongly against the way in which in Prussia the Parliamentary representatives were constrained to grant compensation on the abrogation of exemption from the land taxes, etc. He writes of a Bill, introduced by the Prussian Government, in 1859, that stipulated for such compensation : " When a Government has the incredible weakness to make such a proposal, it, in doing so, virtually renounces its right of sovereignty over the State, and if a Parliament could so far forget its duty as to entertain such a proposal out of consideration for this weakness, it would at least be acting far more logically if it there and then reproclaimed the serfdom of the people to the land-owning nobility." (I., p. 210.) What would Lassalle have said had anyone told him that thirty years later such " weakness," and such " dereliction of duty," would yet be valued national institutions in Prussia ! It is true that at this time Lassalle was still sufficiently naïve to write, that when the Corn Laws were repealed in England, the Tories had not been so " shameless " as "to turn their investments in land—now unprofitable—into a right to compensation in the face of public opinion." (I., p. 208.) Had he lived until our day he would have learnt that what the Tories lacked in 1846 was nothing but the really " practical Christianity," which in modern Germany demands protective duties on corn, enactments that may fetter the agricultural labourer to the soil of the landowner, and the like, as the divine right of the large landlords. But what an irony of history that the work of bringing out the second edition of the " System of Acquired Rights " should have devolved upon none other than Herr Lothar Bucher, the faithful Adlatus of Prince Bismarck, a proficient in the art of " turn-

The well-known Conservative Professor of Jurisprudence, Stahl, had laid down that no age was capable of sitting in judgment upon the past, or the laws emanating therefrom, and of accepting or repudiating these according to its decision as to their suitability. To this Lassalle replies that the first part of the proposition is right, but the second very wrong. The deduction from the first part of the proposition is rather that every age is autonomous, that no age is under the domination of others, and that consequently no age "could be justly bound to perpetuate in itself what is contrary to *its* sense of right, and which must, therefore, be henceforth regarded by it as a wrong instead of a right." (I., p. 173.) But, Lassalle continues, it is not absolutely essential that a people shall have expressed its new idea of right, its new will in words, through the mouth of its representatives. "For to the concept of right it is only necessary that the public opinion of the people shall have informed the sphere of right, *i.e.* actuality, with a spiritual content as the substance of its own will. Under certain given circumstances, however, this may be done as definitely and as energetically, not by words, but by the actual demolition, undertaken by a people of an existing right." (I., p. 380.) This principle had already been laid down by the Roman jurists, and the French Legislation during and *after* the French Revolution had re-affirmed it. History itself had justified the Convention, and historians—even the reactionary ones—had been obliged to approve its action in dating the legal decrees of the French

ing rights of compensation against public opinion." Truly, we can but hope that in a future edition his "professional occupations" will not prevent Herr Lothar Bucher, the literary heir of Lassalle, from "demonstrating" how the "System of Acquired Rights" might have been used or applied during the legislative discussions of recent years. (See the Preface to 2nd Edition.) [The full significance of the latter portion of this note will not be quite grasped by all English readers. It refers to a very dark episode in the history of modern Germany, and I do not propose to wash the dirty linen of others in public. Nevertheless, I feel bound to say in this volume what has just been said, and I must refer the reader who desires more information on the subject to the history of the Protective Duties and Taxation of Spirits in Germany.]

Revolution from the 14th July, 1789, the day of the taking of
the Bastille. And again Lassalle illustrates this by analogous
occurrences in Prussia. He shows how in contradistinction to the
French jurisprudence, the Prussian Higher Court by verbal
quibbling, in several of its sentences evaded the new sense of
right, created by the March Revolution, and expressly acknowledged in the Prussian Constitution, " that all Prussians are equal
before the law, and no class privileges shall obtain," and how, in
a word, it had proved itself a veritable " convention of reaction.'
Four years after the " System " had appeared, this worthy tribunal, by its notorious interpretation of Art. 84 of the Prussian Constitution, proved even to "Liberal calves-heads " how thoroughly
it deserved the title bestowed upon it by Lassalle.

We have seen that acquired rights (1) must be brought about
by individual acts of the Will ; (2) must be in harmony with the
ascertained and expressed *Volks-geist.* This is, in brief, the *theory*
of acquired rights. When, therefore, the French Convention
declared in its decree of the 17th Nivose, Year II. (6th January,
1794), that all the prescriptions of this law, which abolished inheritance by entail, etc., should apply to *all* inheritances entered
upon since the 14th July, 1789, the Convention, according to
Lassalle, in no way violated the principle of acquired rights. On
the contrary, the Convention was fully justified when, on the 22nd
Ventose of the same year, it replied to several petitions presented
on the subject, that this law "had only given expression to the
principle proclaimed by a great people which was again taking
possession of its rights on that day, *i.e.,* on the 14th July, 1789,"
but that the principle of non-retroaction " was not even touched "
by the law, and that this would only become retroactive if this
limit were overstepped, *i.e.,* if the law were made to apply to all
inheritances entered upon before the 14th July, 1789.

From this it is obvious, to return once again to the question of
the law of inheritance, what Lassalle was driving at in his
inquiries into the Roman and Germanic laws of inheritance. The
Roman law of inheritance, based upon the testament and intestate
inheritance, not of the family, but of "groups in which a common

Will was embodied," was, in Rome, an acquired right, because it corresponded with the Roman *Volks-geist*, the "substance" of the Roman people, that is the Idea of the immortality of the subjective Will. In the same way the old Germanic law of inheritance—intestate inheritance of the family—was an acquired right, because it corresponded with an idea of the old Germanic *Volks-geist*, that of the family based upon "the moral identity of its members," of the family which has for its "actual basis the conscious unity of the spirit or love." The family inherits because property generally is only family property. The law of intestacy to-day, however, now that property has become purely individual property, is "no longer based upon the family inheriting as by its own right, nor upon the family as named by the presumed Will of the dead, but upon the family as a *State Institution*," upon "the universal Will of the State regulating the bequeathing of property." (II., p. 500.) And the latter also applies to testamentary right, which, we have seen, is to-day a "compact theoretical impossibility." Neither intestate inheritance nor testamentary right to-day is a natural right, but "the regulating of bequest on behalf of Society." And Lassalle concludes his work with a reference to Leibnitz, who, although he had not grasped the full significance of the testament, yet pronounced the profound apothegm : "Testamento vero mero jure nullius essent momenti, nisi anima esset immortalis "—" But testaments would be, in strict law, null and void if the soul were not immortal."

After this we surely need no special explanation of what Lassalle means, when, controverting Hegel's view of the Testament, he exclaims : "And soon, perchance, it will be shown that from our objective exposition, quite other, and possibly even more radical conclusions as to modern testamentary right will follow." (II., p. 487.) Whatever is not based upon a natural right, but is merely a State institution, the State or Society can at any time alter, curtail or entirely abolish, as seems good for the needs of Society. So that when George Brandes and others following his lead, declare they have not " found a single line " in the whole " System of Acquired Rights " that points to a translation of

Lassalle's theory of inheritance into practice, we cannot but heartily agree with them. It is not a single line, but—to speak as Lassalle would have done—the whole work that cries out for such a translation. Two years later, therefore, when Lassalle was leading the agitation of the General German Working-men's Association, and was accused by the Liberals and Progressists of being an agent of the reactionary party, a correspondent of a Progressist paper warned the Progressist Party against under-valuing Lassalle, the correspondent was quite right in saying, "that Lassalle's 'System of Acquired Rights' contains all the elements from which can be deduced the practice of abolished rights."

What else could Lassalle have meant when he begins his preface by declaring that if his work really solved its problem, it should and could ultimately result in nothing less than "the working out in a scientific juridical sense of the politico-social concept underlying our whole period."

But did Lassalle solve his problem?

So far as his theory of " Acquired Rights " is concerned, its fundamental idea seems pretty generally accepted to-day. Nor can we see what could be advanced against it, even from the Conservative side, now that since 1866, *e.g.*, the proprietary rights of several families have—on the ground of "the many sub-divisions in the German *Volks-geist*,"[1] to quote Lassalle again, (See I., p. 222)—been declared forfeited, although this property had been " acquired " by individual acts of the Will.

But, on the other hand, Lassalle's application of his theory is more questionable, at least, if his example of the nature of the Roman and Germanic law of inheritance is to be taken as its standard. We have already shown the reasons of this weakness, and here we need, therefore, simply recapitulate. Lassalle derives the law of inheritance from the specific *Volks-geist*. Now, although the intimate connection between the system of inheritance and the *Volks-geist* is undeniable, yet this connection is not one

---

[1] Lassalle is here referring to the thirty or more sovereign dynasties then existing in Germany.

of cause and effect. System of inheritance and *Volks-geist* are two effects of one and the same underlying cause, or group of causes. Both are, in the last instance, the product or the expression of the actual conditions of life of a people, growing out of and changing with these, *i.e.*, the law of inheritance is changed as soon as it becomes incompatible with the material conditions of life of a people. Then the *Volks-geist* discovers that a law of inheritance no longer corresponds with its sense of right. And it is the same with all other legal institutions. The *Volks-geist* only *appears* to be the court which pronounces sentence upon their existence. As a matter of fact, it is but the executioner of the sentence, the actual court being the material conditions of life of a people, the way in which the people produces the objects it requires.[1]

How then did Lassalle arrive at so essentially erroneous a theory, transcending even the errors of the old jurists and professors of law? The error lies in this: from end to end of his work Lassalle keeps within the sphere of the juridical and philosophical concept, and he carries through his theory with an iron logic that only does the greater damage to his work. Things are to be explained from their " concept "-derivation; their concept-derivation is to lay bare the laws of their development. But things do not conform to concepts: they have their own laws of development.

Unquestionably, Lassalle was a consummate jurist. He was naturally endowed with exceptional aptitude in this direction, and his long years of struggle with the law courts in the Hatzfeld affair helped to develop this quality even more strongly. Whenever a law is to be analysed, a legal proposition is to be

[1] Of course this relation must not be taken too mechanically. According to the law of action and reaction, all the religious, legal, etc., conceptions, everything, in a word, that one understands by the concept of *Volks-geist*, may again, in turn, exercise a great influence upon the form of the relations of production, *e.g.*, they can within certain limits hasten or retard its development. And it is mankind after all who make their own history. But here we have to do with the final causes that underlie historical development.

followed out to the most intimate depths of its concept, Lassalle
is in his element, and the result absolutely brilliant. But his
strength is also his weakness. The lawyer side in him outweighs
all the rest. And so he looks upon social problems mostly with
the eye of the lawyer. We see this already in his "System of
Acquired Rights"; it constitutes the weakness of that work. We
shall see it later in his socialist agitation.

The "System," together with its Preface, was to be a criticism
of the Hegelian philosophy of jurisprudence. But he only criticises
the latter upon its side issues, takes only a half step forward, while
in the main he keeps to the same standpoint, the same ground as it
does. This is the more remarkable that the step, which should
have been taken in order to make the criticism a really complete
one, had been pointed out long since, and that, too, in works all of
which were known to Lassalle. In an essay, which, moreover, bore
the title, "A Criticism of the Hegelian Philosophy of Right," Marx
had referred to this in the "Deutsch-französisschen Jahrbücher" of
1844. In 1846, in his book on "La Misère de la Philosophie,"
he had clearly outlined it. In 1847, Marx and Engels had shown
its practical application in the "Communist Manifesto." Finally,
in the Preface to his work "Zur Kritik der Politischen Œkonomie,"[1]
(1859), Karl Marx, referring specially to his first essay, had said :
"My investigation"—an investigation to which this essay was but
the introduction—"is summed up in the conclusion that legal
relations and political forms are to be conceived neither
from themselves nor from the so-called universal development
of the human mind, but are found to be rooted in the economic
life conditions. . . . It is not man's consciousness that determines
his being, but, on the contrary, his social being that determines
his consciousness." And although Lassalle was already acquainted
with this book while he was still working at his "System," although
he speaks in the most enthusiastic terms about it to Marx,[2] there
is not a single line in Lassalle's book that could be interpreted in

---

[1] "A Criticism of Political Economy."
[2] In a letter on the 11th September, 1860, he calls it a "masterpiece"
that has "moved him to the profoundest admiration."

the sense of the above. Ought Lassalle to be reproached on this account ? That would be in the highest degree absurd. I note it for the purpose of criticising his standpoint, his method of conception. This, at the time, was still the ideologue-juridical one, as may be seen from his epistolary discussions with Marx on the theory of the law of inheritance set forth in the " System of Acquired Rights."

It is abundantly clear from the above that Marx was bound to oppose Lassalle's conclusions, since these were diametrically opposed to his own theoretical standpoint. What he replied to Lassalle can only be imperfectly gathered from Lassalle's letters to Marx, but this much may be deduced, that the debate, which for the rest was not long carried on by letter, turned essentially upon Lassalle's assertion that the Testament was only to be explained by Roman mythology, the Roman Idea of immortality, and that bourgeois economic development could never by itself have evolved the Testament unless it had found it ready to hand in the Roman law. And it is very characteristic to see how Lassalle, replying to questions put by Marx, and dealing with economic development, always ends by giving his answers an ideologue-juridical turn. The fundamental difference of the theoretical starting-points of the two thinkers comes out most strikingly in this correspondence.

And yet, to repeat it once again, the " System of Acquired Rights," in spite of the false standpoint of his theory of history, remains a very notable achievement, and even for those who do not accept Lassalle's theoretic standpoint, a very suggestive and delightful work.

CHAPTER V.

DURING 1860 and 1861, Lassalle was much taken up with the idea of starting a democratic paper on a large scale in Berlin. We have already seen what he thought of the Liberal press, and we have also seen how anxious he was to be able to immediately influence the course of events in Germany. As a general amnesty was probable at the death of Frederick William IV., Lassalle applied to Marx, asking if he and Engels would, in this event, be inclined to return to Germany, and to bring out such a paper with him.

" In my last letter but one," he writes to Marx on 11th March, " I asked if you two would, in the event of the King's death and the proclamation of a general amnesty, come back and bring out a paper here ? Do answer about this. For I am, on the chance of this, cherishing a hope—still vague and indefinite, it is true—of then bringing out (here in Berlin) a *big* paper along with you. In such an event would you two be inclined to come over ? And how much capital would a *big* paper require ? Would 10,000 thalers, if one could scrape them together, be enough ? Or how much ? I should be glad if you would write to me about this, for I like thinking of this *Chateau en Espagne !* " In the following letters he frequently returns to this idea, and on the 19th January, 1861, when the accession of the new King of Prussia had, in fact, led to an amnesty, he writes more pressingly : " *Once more I ask you* (1) how much capital *must* we have to start a paper here ? (2) Who of the former editors of the *Neue Rheinische Zeitung* would eventually come back here for this purpose ? "

Although Marx yielded to Lassalle's importunities and visited

91

him in the spring of 1861 in Berlin, the plan fell through. To begin with, Lassalle laid down the extraordinary condition that in the editing of the paper he should have one vote, while Marx and Engel, together were also to have only one, as he " would otherwise always be in the minority ! " Then, too, the Prussian Government interpreted the amnesty in such a fashion that those political refugees, who by over ten years' sojourn abroad had forfeited their claim as members of the Prussian Confederation, would by no means benefit directly. They would, on the contrary, be treated exactly in the same way as foreigners seeking naturalisation. And this would have applied to the majority of the refugees, and it would, therefore, have depended upon the pleasure of the Government to " get rid of " anyone whose return might be " inconvenient." And so, of course, a demand for naturalisation for Marx presented by Lassalle was refused, on the ground—according to the reply from the *Liberal* minister of Schwerin to Lassalle, dated 11th November, 1861—that " at the present time, at any rate, there were no special reasons for giving a permit of naturalisation to the said Marx." With this, of course, all idea of Marx' migration to Berlin was knocked on the head.

Towards the end of the summer of 1861, Lassalle made a journey to Italy with the Countess Hatzfeld, a journey which, he writes to Marx, " was most instructive for him." His stay at Caprera with Garibaldi had been most interesting, and he had become acquainted with " almost all the leading people " in the various towns he had visited. In his " Enthüllungen über das tragische Lebensende Ferdinand Lassalle's,"[1] Bernhard Becker declares that Lassalle tried to persuade Garibaldi to make a volunteer invasion of Vienna, and although Becker is by no means scrupulously veracious, the affair, improbable as it appears at first sight, does not seem to have been a mere invention. Moreover, Lassalle had a decided hankering after personal acquaintance with the celebrities of the day. Only this is remarkable. That while, besides Garibaldi, he met all sorts of Italian personages, a few calumnious remarks by Italians sufficed to make him avoid

[1] " Revelations as to the tragic death of Ferdinand Lassalle."

the German Republican and Socialist, Johann Philipp Becker, to
whom Marx had given him a letter of introduction. "Most of
them "—the Italians—" don't know him at all," Lassalle writes
to "inform" Marx about Becker. "Those who do know him
think him a *blagueur* and loafer and HUMBUG. . . He is only on
good terms with Turr, who is certainly a creature of Napoleon's,
dependent upon his purse." In consequence he had determined not
to make use of Marx' letter of introduction. "You know how
often we are so placed when abroad, that we avoid nothing so
carefully as our own countrymen." Now the excellent Johann
Philipp was, at all events, not an ordinary swaggerer, but one
who had again and again stood out manfully for the cause of
freedom, and a meeting with him Lassalle might well have put
up with. And when, later on, he started the General German
Working men's Association, he knew how to find Becker's address,[1] and writing to the latter—who had somehow heard of the
rumours current about him—represented the matter in such a
light as if it had been Marx, who, making a mountain out of a
mole-hill, had placed upon a casu l remark about Becker's intercourse with Turr so evil a construction.

It was not until the January of 1862 that Lassalle returned to
Berlin. He found the political situation essentially changed.
The differences between the King of Prussia and Liberal middle-
classdom had grown into an open conflict. At the recent
Parliamentary election, in the beginning of December, 1861, the
weak-kneed Constitutional Party had been ousted through the
rather more determined tone adopted by the Progressist Party.
The latter had, during the summer of the same year, grown from
the party—until then a small minority in the Chamber—of the
"Yung Lithauen," or rather had formed around these as an
nucleus. But the Progressist Party was by no means homogeneous. It consisted of the most diverse elements : persons of
the upper middle-class with a leaning towards Liberalism sat in it

---

[1] That the Italian leaders knew Becker very well is shown by a letter of
Mazzini to Becker in June, 1861. See Rüegg's "Extracts from the Papers
of Joh. Ph. Becker," published in the *Neue Zeit* for 1888, p. 458, etc.

side by side with petty bourgeois democrats; ex-republicans, with milk and water socialistic tendencies, side by side with men who were more royalist than the King himself. With Hohenzollern obstinacy, William I. had managed to fall out with all of them; only the party of the squires and the bigots, and the actual bureaucracy with their following, stood by the Government. The Progressist Party commanded the large majority of the Chamber, and almost the whole of public opinion in the country. Even people who saw through the real nature of this party, and who were too radical to become members of it, thought it wise not to oppose it at that time, but rather to wait and see how it would carry on its struggle with the Prussian Government.

For some time already, Lassalle had fallen out with the chief men of the Progressist Party in Berlin. Yet, at the beginning of 1860, in a letter to Marx, he had broken a lance with very great, if altogether uncalled for, vehemence for the Berlin *Volks Zeitung;* had called it a paper which "even though with much less courage than was necessary, and with much less determination than, despite the enslavement of the press, it should have shown, had on the whole defended through all these years, and still was defending, the democratic standpoint." And he had declared every other policy than that pursued by the *Neue Rheinische Zeitung* in 1848 towards the "blue-revolutionary" [1] papers and parties, to be "as false theoretically as pernicious practically." With regard to the "*vulgär democratischen*" parties and their different shades of opinion, he writes : "We must hold as fast to the *identity* as to the *difference* of our social revolutionary standpoint as compared with theirs. There will be time enough to show *only* the difference when they are victorious." And should the party in London, on the other hand, have arrived at the decision to treat all merely "blue-revolutionary" papers and parties alike, "then I declare most distinctly that I shall not follow them in this transmutation, but shall rather everywhere combat it *à outrance.*"

Nevertheless, in his letter of the 19th January, 1861, he informs Marx that he had taken advantage of the refusal of the

[1] As contrasted with the advanced "red-revolutionists."

Volks Zeitung to insert a long article of his against the *National Zeitung* as an excuse for breaking with its editor, Franz Dunker. " Breaking off our acquaintance, I mean, for there was nothing else whatever. I am taking advantage of the excuse, I say, for it is to me more a desired opportunity than a reason. I had long come to see the necessity of this with regard to him. One can't have anything to do with these faint-hearted creatures, so I shall take advantage of this to break off all connection with him—as I should have done long ago, but for my constitutional good nature." And so, in the Preface to the " System of Acquired Rights," dated March 27th, 1861, we already find an attack, in this place indeed somewhat uncalled for, upon the " spokesmen of the liberal bourgeoisie," whose " conception of politics is one of supine dulness and superficiality," of " isolation " that forces them to lose themselves in mere words, and to fight *about* words, *with* words, *for* words. Nevertheless, Lassalle still kept up his relations with other Progressist and National Liberals, and in Berlin itself, the only immediate result of the rupture with Dunker was that ever more and more equivocal personages formed Lassalle's circle of acquaintance. With the exception of a few real *savants*, quite ordinary society lions, like Baron Korff, Meyerbeer's son-in-law, or artists playing at Radicalism, like Hans von Bülow,[1] etc., could boast of intimate friendship with Lassalle. In her "Apology," Frau Helene von Racowitza describes—unintentionally, it is true, but

---

[1] Lassalle's Letters to Hans von Bülow were published in the eighties (Dresden and Leipzig, H. Minden). The editing is as slovenly as the volume is small. In the Preface, a passage from a letter of Heine's about Lassalle is ascribed to Prince Pückler-Muskau. The letters themselves are not even chronologically arranged. The non-dating of his letters by Lassalle is, no doubt, the excuse for this, although the dates of most of them could have easily been fixed by their contents. In one of the letters, " Salinger's genial composition " is spoken of. The editor, who had got the letters from Herr Hans von Bülow himself, adds to this as a note, " Workers' Hymn by Herwegh." That the name of Salinger, *i.e.*, Solinger, was a pseudonym of Hans von Bülow is, on the other hand, not so much as hinted at. Was this modesty or—remorse on the part of the inspirer of the publication ?

therefore all the more effectively—the very mixed, and to some
extent very rotten, society in which Lassalle lived, when she made
his acquaintance in the beginning of 1862. Of the Advocate
Hiersemenzel, at whose house the first meeting between Helene
and Lassalle took place, and whose "charming fair-haired wife"
pointed out Lassalle to her as one of her husband's most intimate
friends, Lassalle himself wrote a few months later—on the 2nd
June, 1862—to Marx : "By the way, I have broken *for ever*[1] with
that very low pike Hiersemenzel," and he characteristically adds :
"Now, don't run away with the idea that his wife was at the
bottom of it."

The friendship of Lassalle with Herr Lothar Bucher—who after
the amnesty had returned to Germany, and settled down in
Berlin—proved more lasting. Bucher was certainly no "pike,"
but belonged to quite another zoological class.

From a letter of Bucher's to Lassalle, of the 19th January, 1862,
—published in the Berlin *Freie Presse* in the middle of July,
1878—it appears that Lassalle had returned from Italy with some
very venturesome plans. Bucher, who at this time had plenty
of reasons for "hating this old order of the world," at this
time "he was a private individual," later as "privy-councillor," in
his Preface to the 2nd Ed. of the "System of Acquired
Rights," put a different gloss upon it. Referring to a discussion
with Lassalle on the previous evening, he declares that he had
certainly thought it possible to overthrow the existing order—"or
disorder"—of things in Germany, but not to keep it down ;
in other words, that the time was not yet ripe for a socialist
revolution. "And pray, consider this also, that every socialist movement in France will yet for a long time to come be
impregnated with the dirt and poison of Bonapartism, and that
with us a mass of healthy and pure elements would rise against
such a movement in our midst." To the question, what should
be done then ?—he had but "the lame answer of Machiavelli" :
politics is a choice between evils. "A victory of militarism"
—*i.e., of the Prussian Government !*—would be "an evil,"

----

[1] *For ever* in English in the original.

but "a victory of the Austria of to-day would be a victory of the reactionary principle." As a proof of this, he would refer Lassalle to the *Berlin Revue*, etc. All these objections to arguments advanced by Lassalle allow of only one explanation—that Lassalle believed a revolution could be forced on, and had chosen Austria as its excuse. This, of course, would explain the attempt above referred to, and his trying to win over Garibaldi to a volunteer descent upon Vienna. The only doubtful point is how Lassalle, who was usually in political matters a very prudent calculator, could have taken up so foolhardy a plan. Whether it had been hatched by the Countess Hatzfeld, who was burning to see Lassalle play a public part, or whether it had been suggested by the French, Hungarian or Italian revolutionists whom Lassalle had met on his journey to and through Italy, must remain uncertain. But the plan—well as it fitted in with certain of Lassalle's ideas—can hardly have originated with him.

At any rate, Lassalle, returned home, was convinced that for a revolution in Germany, there were, above all, still wanting German revolutionists. Nevertheless, the situation was too troubled for Lassalle to have the quiet necessary for a return to his literary studies. Instead of immediately setting about the great national economic work he had intended taking up, he again and again put this off, in order to devote himself to questions of the day. And this, with public life becoming daily more keen and pulsating, was certainly natural enough. The first work Lassalle now presented to the public was the pamphlet, written together with Bucher, "Julian Schmidt, der Literar Historiker." [1] Although the work is formally directed against a compilation of Herr Schmidt's : "Geschichte der Deutschen Literatur," [2] the Preface shows that the Liberal press, as a whole, was aimed at in it, and the Liberal Party also. As Herr Julian Schmidt was one of those who had signed the Liberal Programme, "Julian der Grabowite" might fairly be taken as "representing the intellectual culminating

---

[1] "Julian Schmidt, the Historian of Literature."
[2] "History of German Literature."

point of this party." Somewhat exaggerated logic, but, indeed, the whole work abounds in exaggerations.[1]

It is questionable also, whether so mocking an identification was well-timed when the Government had just dissolved the Chamber, and when the King, in his rescript of the 20th March (Lassalle's Preface is dated March 22nd), had called upon the ministers to "make a stand against calumnies, whose object was to confuse unsuspecting public opinion," and when the struggle between the popular representatives and the Government was becoming acute. On the whole, however, the lesson read Herr Schmidt was well deserved, the severe castigation of mental inertia, posing in "the pompous language of culture," thoroughly justified. The wit is rather forced, but then again an apt quotation from the classics often makes up for this. Where "the compositor" makes remarks, it is always Lassalle who speaks ; Lothar Bucher figures as "the compositor's wife."[2]

In the spring of 1862, an invitation to lecture to one of the Berlin Ward Liberal Clubs, gave Lassalle the opportunity—denied him in the press—of meeting the leaders of the Progressist Party face to face, before their own followers. He took for his subject the question of the day : the constitutional conflict which was raging. In his first lecture, which he called, "On Constitutions in General," however, he with shrewd calculation confined himself

[1] Just as it is not wanting in strained assumptions. Oddly enough, too, Lassalle allows the "compositor's wife" to reproach Herr Schmidt with various sins, which he, of all men, had good reasons for judging leniently. When, *e.g.*, Schmidt speaks of Uhland's protest, in 1848, against the more closely federated State (*i.e.*, against *Klein Deutschland*), and of the figure used by Uhland, that in the voice of every Austrian deputy he heard the murmur of the Adriatic, as showing a want of comprehension of the historical situation, he might have taken, as proof for this, Lassalle's "Italian War and the Mission of Prussia," which represented the non-destruction of Austria as the real cause of the failure of the 1848 Revolution. And in the same way Schmidt might have replied to the reproach of "wild Protestant sound and fury" made by Lassalle-Bucher, by referring to "Franz von Sickingen."

[2] The criticism of Schmidt's book is in the form of notes by the compositor and the compositor's wife.

wholly to an academic exposition. He develops his standpoint of principle, without saying anything about its practical consequences. Questions of constitution are questions of power; a constitution has only an assured existence when and so long as it is the expression of real conditions of power. A people is only protected against the arbitrariness of its rulers, so long as it is in a position, and is determined to protect itself in the ultimate issue against such arbitrariness even without the constitution. Thus the greatest mistake in 1848 had been, that instead of at the outset changing the real factors of power, of, above all, transforming the army from a royalist into a popular one, so much time was wasted in the working out of a constitution, that the counter-revolution had gathered sufficient strength to disband the National Assembly. Should the people again be in a position to make a constitution, they must take this lesson to heart. The Army Bill brought in by the Government must also be considered from this point of view—*i.e.*, as a result of the wish to turn actual conditions to account for the Government. " Royalty, gentlemen," he says in conclusion, " has practical servants, not phrasemongers, and such practical servants as you yourselves might wish to have."

The fundamental idea from which Lassalle here starts is indisputably correct. And most of the Progressists knew it. If, in spite of this, they pretended to have a different standpoint, they did this because the translation of the former into practice simply meant the Revolution, while the Progressist Party desired—a portion of it as final aim, the rest, at any rate, for the time being —to carry on the struggle on parliamentary lines. But one hardly needed to be such a deadly enemy of the Revolution, as Lassalle represented the Progressists—though with regard to a considerable proportion of them rightly enough—to consider the time for such a Revolution not yet ripe. And as we have seen, Lassalle's friend, Bucher, despite his manifold reasons for hating the existing order of things, was of this opinion. But for a parliamentary struggle, the fiction that one was fighting for the existing constitution against the Government that had violated it, was fighting for Right against Might, provided a far more favourable, or rather let us say, a far more convenient position than the open declaration of war for supremacy could have done. All material means of power were in the hands of the Government, and so one at least wanted to make sure of the moral means.

Although Lassalle had said nothing in his lecture that any Progressist—or, for the matter of that, any sensible being—could object to, yet on that very account he was extremely obnoxious to the leaders of the Progressist Party, while the governmental and reactionary parties rubbed their hands with delight. The *Kreuz-Zeitung*, the organ of the Squirearchy and Church, sang his praises quite openly. The *Kreuz-Zeitung* was glad not merely to see the conflict carried into the heart of the enemy, it was also anxious to have the question of the Constitution represented as nothing but a question of supremacy between the monarchy and the popular representatives, because its position as the only reliable pillar of the throne would thus become more secure. Nor must we forget that the "new era" of William I. had also been, among other things, an attempt to emancipate the Hohenzollern throne from the now galling yoke of the squirearchy east of the Elbe, and of the bureaucracy. Yet this, compared with the programme as formulated by Lassalle, must undoubtedly seem the lesser evil to the King.

"By special request," Lassalle published this lecture, which he had repeated at three other Progressist meetings—a proof that the Progressist electors saw nothing questionable about it. In the meantime the elections to the Landtag had resulted in a brilliant victory of the Progressists over the Government, and everyone was waiting with bated breath to see how, under these conditions, the conflict between the two would work out further.

In the spring of 1862, Lassalle also gave a second lecture in Berlin—in the Artisans' Club of the Oranienburger suburb, the engineers' quarter of Berlin. He called it: "On the Special Connection between the Idea of the Working-class Estate and the Present Historical Period." This second lecture also he had carefully prepared. And if it is not altogether above criticism in

certain details—its very title provokes criticism—it is yet one of
the best, if not the best, of Lassalle's speeches. Language as
clear as it is beautiful; argument terse, flowing, nowhere extra-
vagant, and yet never dry ; a systematic, progressive development
of the fundamental idea, from proposition to proposition, are its
excellencies of manner; while its matter—with, as we have said, some
exceptions—may be taken as an excellent introduction into the
world of thought of Socialism. And it in nowise detracts from its
value if I call this speech a paraphrase of the " Communist Manifesto," adapted to the time and circumstances under which it was
delivered. In the main it develops in detail what the Manifesto,
in its historical portion, had already laid down on broad lines.

It is true that Hegelian ideology and the juridical point of view
still run through the argument, but along with these the note of
the economic basis of history is also sounded. That the working-
class, thanks to its class conditions in modern bourgeois society, is
the really revolutionary class, the class destined to place Society
upon a new basis—the fundamental idea of the "Communist
Manifesto,"—is also the leading idea of the " Arbeiter Programm,"[1]
under which title the lecture was subsequently published. Only
for Lassalle, this principle at once crystallises into juridical concepts, and becomes impregnated with ideological notions. Lassalle's
constant use, both in the title and all through his lecture, of the
term " Arbeiterstand," (working-class estate), might be looked
upon as a mere concession to a common phrase, to which only a
pedant could take exception. To his honour it must, however,
be said, that Lassalle never set about his choice of words lightly.
It was not a mere acceptance of a popular phrase that induced
him to speak of the " working-class estate," of the " fourth estate,"
but rather the consequence of his essentially juridical point of
view. It is the same reversion to the juridical method that
makes him derive the concept of the bourgeois not from the
actual power which the possession of capital confers, and which is
due solely to its economic effects and forces, but from the juridical
and political privileges which the bourgeois enjoys or claims on

[1] " Worker's Programme."

the strength of his property. Instead of clearly pointing out the
fundamental difference between the modern bourgeois and the
feudal lord of the Middle-Ages, he, on the contrary, obliterates it,
and only then admits that the possessor of capital becomes a
bourgeois when he lays claim to the State and legal position of a
feudal lord. (See pp. 20-22, " Arbeiter Programm," 1st Edition.)
And, as always, logical even in his error, Lassalle represents the
class or census electoral system as the distinctive feature of
bourgeois society, represents it, that is, not as *a*, but as *the* distinctive feature. The Prussian three-class electoral system, introduced by the feudal-absolutist reaction against the bourgeois
Revolution of 1848, is, according to him, the electoral system of
the modern bourgeois State. This may, perhaps, have some
meaning if the concept bourgeois is confined to the few large
capitalists *à la* Stumm, but then what becomes of the " fourth
estate " ?

As a further characteristic of the bourgeois State thus defined,
Lassalle takes the development of the system of indirect taxation
as a means for shifting the burden of the taxes upon the non-
privileged classes. That every privileged class has the tendency
to free itself as far as possible from taxation, may pass uncon-
tested, but when Lassalle makes the concept of the class-state
depend upon the existence of electoral rights, his theory is at once
vitiated by the simple fact that in the very country where direct
and universal franchise has longest existed, the system of indirect
taxation is most completely developed. Very questionable also
is Lassalle's deduction that of the 97 million thalers paid
to the Prussian State in taxes, in the year 1855, only some
13 million resulted from direct taxation. He calmly declares the
10 million thalers of land tax an indirect tax, on the ground that
it is not paid by the owners of the land, but is shifted by them on
to the price of corn. This shifting was, however, by no means
an easy matter, so long as the frontiers had not been closed
against importations from abroad by means of Protectionist duties.
For a long time, indeed, the land tax did affect landed property
as a fixed charge ; such, too, it was felt to be by the landed pro-

prietors, and as such it was treated in cases of alienation. Nine million thalers' revenue from law costs might be called indirect taxes, but as the poorest class is by no means the one that most enters into litigation, one cannot—whatever else one may think of the law costs—speak of it as a tax for the relief of the great capitalist. In short, the relative exemption from taxation of the great capitalists is not necessarily a criterion of bourgeois society. This last, indeed, differs from feudal society, by the fact that it is not bound to legalised class-differences by statute, but rather continues to exist in spite of the formal equality of all before the law.

Lassalle is more correct when he cites the enforced depositing of newspaper " caution "-money and the newspaper stamp-duty as a proof that " the bourgeoisie maintains the supremacy of its own peculiar privilege and element—*i.e ,* of capital—with even severer logic than did the nobles in the Middle-Ages, with regard to landed property." Newspaper " caution "-money, and the newspaper stamp-duty were, in Prussia, by no means governmental measures of the bourgeoisie, but of the semi-feudal and bureaucratic reaction. Lassalle need only have turned to England, where the bourgeoisie had reached the highest point of development, in order to convince himself that, even without the petty measures of a retrograde system of government, the press may become, and that to a greater extent than in Prussia, " a privilege of the great capitalist." Right as it of course was to speak out against the methods of political repression, it is yet another proof of Lassalle's juridical bent of mind, that when he wishes to depict the effect of bourgeois supremacy upon the condition of the press, he refers *exclusively* to formal legal institutions, and absolutely ignores the influence of the economic factors. Finally, his ideology leads him to sing pæan to the State, to the " Concept of the State." The " fourth estate " has " quite another, quite a different conception of the ethical aim of the State from the bourgeoisie."

The State-concept of the bourgeoisie, Lassalle declares, is that of the Liberal Free-Trade School, according to which the sole

function of the State is to protect the personal freedom and property of the individual.

But this, he says, is a " night-watchman idea." [1]   History is "a
struggle with Nature ; with the misery, the ignorance, the
poverty, the helplessness, and, therefore, with the enslavement of
all kinds that hemmed us in when the human race first appeared
at the beginning of History.   A progressive *victory* over this helplessness—that is the development of freedom that History shows
us."   To accomplish the development of the human race towards
freedom, *this* is the true mission of the State.   The State is " the
unity of individuals in an ethical whole," its object being " to make
it possible for the individuals, by means of this unity, to attain such
ends, such a stage of existence, as they as individuals never could
attain ; to enable them to attain a degree of culture, power, and
freedom, that would be, to every one of them as individuals, absolutely
unattainable."   And further, the object of the State is "to bring man
to positive expansion and progressive development, in other
words, to fashion the human *destiny—i.e.*, the culture of which
the human race is capable—into actual being;" it is "the education
and development of man to freedom."   So clearly is this " the true
and higher mission " of the State that this mission " has been
more or less carried out by the State through all time, by the
force of circumstance, and even without its own will, even unconsciously, even against the will of its leaders."

And the working-class " estate," the lower classes of Society
generally, thanks to the helpless position in which its members,
as individuals, are placed, had " the profound instinct that
this is, and must be, the destiny of the State."   And a State
dominated by the idea of the working-class estate, would make
this " moral nature " of the State its mission, " with the clearest
perception and complete consciousness," and " would bring about
an elevation of thought, the development of a sum of happiness,

---

[1] Lassalle here refers to the idea of the Manchester School (of Germany),
that the duties of Government were not to exceed those of a constable of
the watch.

culture, well-being, and freedom, unparalleled in the history of the world."

This interpretation contains a great error in relation to the historical moment : despite all the emphasis laid upon the historical changes of State and of Society, the State itself is represented as being in its concept and essence one for all time, as having had from the beginning a definite aim underlying its " idea," an "idea" occasionally misunderstood, only partially understood, or entirely ignored, and which must therefore be helped to a complete recognition. The concept of the State is, so to say, an eternal one. In this sense, Lassalle quotes a passage from an address of Bœckh's, in which the celebrated antiquarian appeals from " the State-concept of Liberalism," to the " antique culture " which has now, once for all, become the inalienable foundation of the German mind, and which has given birth to the idea that the concept of the State must be so far enlarged that " *the State shall be the institution in which the whole virtue of mankind shall realise itself.*" Comprehensible, and, within certain limits, justifiable as was this protest against the theory, at that time so cock-a-hoop, of absolute social and political *laisser aller, laisser faire,* Lassalle here overshot the mark. The " State " of the ancients was based upon conditions of society differing so fundamentally from those of the present time, that the ideas of the ancients about the State are as little applicable to the present time as their ideas about labour, money, and the family. Like these ideas, the ancient idea of the State only supplies material for comparative research, not for a theory capable of modern application.

If, according to Bœckh, the State-concept as understood by Liberalism involved the danger of a " modern barbarism," so the grafting upon the society of to-day, of the State-concept as understood by the ancients, involves the danger of a modern State-slavery. Then, too, Lassalle is quite wrong in what he says of the effects of the State. These have, indeed, greatly differed at different periods. Immense strides were made in civilisation before a State existed, and great civilising missions were fulfilled without either help from, or opposition to the State of that time. In the

main, no doubt, the State has aided the advance of mankind, but
it has also often been a hindrance to it.

Of course, Lassalle did not look upon the matter from so unhistorical a standpoint as to desire the restoration of the State-
concept of the ancients unchanged—nor had Bœckh any such idea
either—but the direct derivation of the State-concept from theirs
made matters not better, but worse. The cult of the State as
such, means the cult of every State, and even if Lassalle's
democratic and socialist views made it impossible for him to support directly the existing State, it did not prevent this cult from
being exploited later on by the advocates of the existing State in
its interest.   Indeed, the Achilles heel of all ideology, of all
theory built upon preconceived concepts, is that, no matter how
revolutionary in intention, they are really always in danger of being transformed into a glorification of existing, or of past institutions.   Lassalle's concept of the State is the bridge that was one
day to bring together the Republican Lassalle and the men fighting for absolute monarchy, the Revolutionist Lassalle and the out-
and-out reactionaries.   Philosophical absolutism has at all times
had a tendency inclining it to political absolutism.

Thus this lecture, despite its merits, in other respects contains
in germ all those errors that came out in the subsequent Lassallean
movement.

In conclusion, Lassalle exhorts the workers to steep themselves
in the thought of the great historical mission of their class, and
to find in it the duty of taking up an entirely new position.
" The vices of the oppressed, the idle indifference of the thoughtless, and even the harmless frivolity of the small-minded, no longer
become you now.   *You* are the rock upon which the Church of
the present is to be built ! "

As I have said, Lassalle had this lecture printed.   Cautious as
he had been, carefully as he avoided drawing any immediate
political conclusions, the Berlin police—especially as Lassalle's
political views were well known to them—at once scented what
the lecture was really driving at.   They seized the whole edition
of 3000 copies brought out by a Berlin publisher, and instituted

criminal proceedings against Lassalle. The pamphlet had appeared, and had been confiscated at the end of June. On the 4th November, 1862, the Public Prosecutor, Von Schelling—a son of the philosopher Schelling—applied to the Berlin *Stadtgericht* for permission to proceed against Lassalle for " exciting the non-possessing classes to hatred and contempt of the possessing class." On the 17th November, the Court decided to grant the request, and on the 16th January, 1863, the case came before the Court of the First Instance. In spite of a truly brilliant defence, in which Lassalle proved himself superior both to the Crown Attorney and to the President of the Court, and in which he especially flagellated the former, he was sentenced to four months' imprisonment. He appealed, and had at least this satisfaction, that the *Kammergericht* commuted the sentence of imprisonment to one of a comparatively small fine. The confiscation of the pamphlet was certainly upheld, but Lassalle in the meantime had a new edition published by Meyer and Zeller at Zürich.

Meyer and Zeller also published the three pamphlets on the trial before the Court of First Instance. Of these pamphlets the first consisted of Lassalle's Defence, (published under the separate title of " Die Wissenschaft and die Arbeiter " [1]); the second, the verbatim report of the pleadings at the trial ; and the third, a rather tedious criticism of the sentence of the Court of First Instance ; and finally, under the title of " Die Indirekten Steuern and die Lage der Arbeitenden Klassen," [2] his defence before the Higher Court. We shàll return to the consideration of these pamphlets later on. Here, and now, we must go back to the time in which the lecture itself was delivered, the spring of 1862. It is easy to understand that the speech, as such, should not, at first, have created any particular sensation. Greatly as its actual contents differed from the kind of fare that the Progressist orators were at this time setting before the Berlin workers, its exoteric political tendency differed but little from theirs. Radical phrases, allusions to a new edition of the 1848 Revolution,

[1] " Science and the Workers."
[2] " Indirect Taxation, and the Position of the Working-Classes,"

attacks upon the indirect taxes, etc., were plentiful enough in the speeches of dozens of Progressist democratic orators. Indeed, as the latter interlarded their speeches with denunciations of the Government, these usually sounded far more radical than Lassalle's address, with its almost completely academic form. When the Philistine does side with the opposition, he can bluster with the best of them. As a speech, the "Worker's Programme" did not produce any great effect either upon the workers or upon the middle-class.

And so, in this same spring, Lassalle was elected by the Berlin "Philosophical Society," of which he was a member, to deliver the address at their forthcoming celebration, on the 19th May, of the centenary of the Philosopher Fichte. Neither his social nor his political radicalism, which, of course, were well known in these circles, gave offence at this time. As the majority of middle-classdom was with the opposition, its *savants* also were still allowed to indulge in ideology.

Six months before, in the "Democratic Studies," Lassalle had celebrated Fichte as the Apostle of the German Republic, and to entrust him now with delivering the address at the celebration was really nothing less than a ratification of that essay. And Lassalle took care to turn this opportunity to account, and to repeat what he had then said in another form.

The speech is entitled "Die Philosophie Fichte's, und die Bedeutung des Deutschen Volks-geists."[1] And it is not only in its representation of Fichte's philosophical political ideas that it is entirely ideological. Lassalle himself here again falls into the most approved old Hegelian ideology. The German *Volks-geist* is the metaphysical *Volks-idee* (*i.e.*, National-idea), and its meaning consists in this : that the Germans have the great historical significance of creating for it, from the "pure spirit," "not only a real actuality," but even "the very locality of its existence, its arena. . . . Because here the existence is begotten of the 'pure spirit' itself, intermingled with nothing historical, natural,

[1] "The Philosophy of Fichte, and the Significance of the German *Volks-geist.*"

special, it can only be the actual picture of the pure Thought, and herein bears the necessity of that determination towards the highest and most perfect spirituality of freedom that Fichte predicts for it." And what Fichte had philosophically enunciated in his loneliness as a thinker, this, making good another of his axioms, had already " become a religion," and beat " under the popular and dogmatic name of GERMAN UNITY in every noble German heart."

To represent the striving for German unity as the result of the " pure spirit, intermingled with nothing historical "—this outdid even the ideology of Liberalism. And so it appears that this address, though worked out with rigid logic and consistency of thought, entirely failed to impress the public gathered to hear it. As B. Becker tells us, the audience, to the intense annoyance of Lassalle, gradually left the room (where the speechifying went on) " to make for another, where an appetising meal was spread." Becker forgets to add that the audience did not consist only of members of the Philosophical Society, but chiefly of guests invited by them ; people who, for the most part, attend such meetings because it is " the thing."

Lassalle published this speech also in separate form, and sent it, together with the " Julian Schmidt," and the " Lecture on the Essence of the Constitution," through Lothar Bucher to Marx. He had " begun a little of practical political agitation," he writes, on the 9th June, to Marx. " Thus I delivered the Constitution speech to *four* associations. And, besides, I have written a much longer address on the Worker's Estate, and delivered it before a workman's club." This is the " Worker's Programme." " And I have now made up my mind," he adds, " to have it published ; it is already in the press. As soon as it is ready I'll send it you." Later on in the letter he again refers to the fact, that owing to his intense pre-occupation with other things during the last three years, the national-economic matters in his mind had become " well-nigh fossilised." Not until " it had all become fluid again " would he proceed to a second reading of Marx' book, " A Criticism of Political Economy," and at the same time to a review of it, and to the carrying out of his own economic work—" this LAST, it is true, will take a very long time." Moreover, this programme would, in any case, be interrupted by a two months' journey, as he could not stand a summer in Berlin. In July he would go to Switzerland, or come to London first, and then go to Switzerland. He decided in favour of the latter. But before this he once again wrote to Marx :

"DEAR MARX,—The bearer of this is Captain Schweigert, who has served with distinction under Garibaldi, and especially under my friend Rustow. He is the most honest and reliable fellow in the world. C'est un homme d'action. He is at the head of the *Wehr-Vereine* (Arms-Club) that he has organised from Coburg, and is now proceeding to London to try and raise the money for getting 3000 muskets, which he requires for the *Wehr-Vereine.* I've no need to tell you how desirable this would be. So be good enough to put him in communication with people from whom he can obtain money for this purpose, or any kind of assistance towards this end. Do your best. The probability of my coming to London grows.—Thine,

"F. LASSALLE.

"Berlin, 19/6/62."

The *Wehr-Vereine* being organised from Coburg, belonged to the camp of the " National Club," which had its headquarters in that town. It is evident that Lassalle had not yet by any means entirely broken with this Club. His emphasis on the " homme d'action," and his great interest in the acquisition of 3000 muskets are a further confirmation of what has been said above with regard to Lassalle's revolutionary plans.

With two short letters, written in London itself, that refer to visits and to an excursion to be undertaken together, the letters which I have from Lassalle to Marx end. It would, however, be a mistake to conclude from this that the visit to London had led to a rupture between the two. Such a rupture never occurred. But it is very possible that in talking things over with Marx,

Lassalle understood more clearly than he had hitherto done the fundamental difference of the standpoints of the two men. At any rate, after Lassalle's return to Berlin, in the autumn of 1862, the correspondence entirely ceased. All the more closely did Lassalle attach himself to Bucher, who later also brought him into relation with Rodbertus.

At the end of the summer of 1862, it seemed for a moment as if the Prussian Government were going to adopt a more conciliatory attitude towards the Chamber. Negotiations were again carried on until the King suddenly informed the Chamber in the bluntest way that he would not consent to any concessions with regard to the shortening of the term of military service, and that he felt no inclination whatever to recommend a special grant for the unconstitutional procedure with regard to the re-organisation of the army. To this the Chamber replied that by 308 votes to 11 it had rejected the demand of the Government to include the expenditure for the re organisation of the army among the ordinary items of expenditure in the budget. In order to break down the resistance of the majority, the King now summoned the Prussian Ambassador to France, Otto von Bismarck, who was just then in Berlin, to take the place of Herr von der Heydt in the Ministry. In all probability the churlish way in which the King in his message had laid stress upon his sovereign privileges, was the result of an understanding with Bismarck.

Bismarck, who had appeared in the " United Landtag " of 1847, and in the Prussian National Assembly of 1849, as the Hotspur of the feudal squirearchy, had, in the meantime, developed into the " modern statesman." He had thrown his landowner ideologies overboard, in order the more effectually to guard the "consolidated land-owning " interests. He had given up the absolutism proclaimed before the March days, thereby to assure the monarchy an even more advantageous position by saddling the Chamber with the responsibility—and only the responsibility —of the demands of the monarchy. In short, he had adopted the maxims of that system of government known as Bonapartism, which, when it speaks of democracy, means governmental

violence, and which proclaims its care for the well-being of
the poor, when it is meditating a campaign of taxation against
the pockets of the workers. From Russian diplomacy he had
learnt how one can maintain an absolutist Government and
intrigue under the rose with revolutionists; and from French
diplomacy that one must always accuse an opponent of a dishonourable action at the very moment when oneself is contemplating exactly the same action. Besides this, he made a specialty
of the trick of all astute diplomatists and sharpers, of displaying
on certain occasions an astounding " bluntness," so that the
next time they may so much the more successfully make use of
language in order not to speak the truth.

It was with this " bluntness " that Bismarck made his début in
the Chamber, and naturally his German programme was not
believed in. His declaration in the Budget Commission that the
German question would only be solved through " blood and iron,"
merely intensified the opposition. The House stuck to its resolution to vote nothing to the Government until its constitutional
rights had been acknowledged by the latter, whereupon Bismarck
prorogued the House with the declaration that, for the time being,
the Government would take the money wherever they found it.

Meanwhile, Bismarck's position was by no means a very secure
one. He certainly had the force of the Government—*i.e.*, organised
force—at his back, while the Chamber had nothing but " public
opinion " on its side. But he knew perfectly well that he could
not " sit " upon the Prussian bayonettes. Unequivocal success in
his foreign policy, likely to win over the ex-" Gothaer," *i.e.*, the
weak-kneed Kleindeutsch Liberals to the Government, was, for
the time being, not to be reckoned upon. So he had to seek elsewhere for allies against the Progressist party.

It was about this time, in the autumn of 1862, that at various
working-men's clubs, which had either been actually started by the
Progressists, or were supported by them, the notorious " working-
man," Eichler, suddenly appeared. He accused the Progressist
Party of incompetence, and inveighed against the Schulze-Delitzsch
co-operative associations as useless to the workers. The " self-help,"

about which the Liberals were making such a fuss, was no good ; the State alone could help the workers.   Eichler, who declared that his employer had dismissed him on account of his adverse criticism of Schulze's " self-help " ideas, nevertheless found means to travel to Leipzig, where the local Working-men's Club was eagerly discussing the summoning of a General Working-men's Congress for the purpose of founding an independent working-men's organisa‌tion.   He tried to induce the Leipzig Central Committee to call the Congress at Berlin, and on their coming to closer quarters with him, at last, in the heat of the discussion, came out with the declara‌tion, that he knew for certain that the Prussian Government was willing to help the workers, especially with the starting of pro‌ductive co-operative associations.   He could inform them also that Herr von Bismarck was prepared to give 30,000 thalers for start‌ing a productive co-operative machine-making association—the Berlin machine-makers being then, and for a long time after, the picked battalions of the Progressist army !   Of course the workers would have to make up their minds to turn their backs upon the Progressist Party, as this was the party of the bourgeoisie, the greatest enemy of the workers.

In this Herr Eichler failed completely, for the people in Leipzig who were organising the Workers' Congress desired anything rather than to oblige the Prussian Government by attacking the Progressists in the rear.   Herr Eichler went home again without accomplishing his purpose, and seems to have done little in Berlin either.   When called to account for his notoriously luxurious mode of life, which was so little in keeping with an " out-of-work," he made mysterious allusions to a rich aristocratic lady who had taken a fancy to him, and as he was a good-looking fellow, this was not altogether improbable.   Eichler then disappeared from the scene, to turn up later on as a Prussian police official.

When, sixteen years after, at the sitting of the Reichstag of the 16th September, 1878, Bebel twitted Bismarck—meantime made a Prince—with the Eichler " mission," Bismarck, the next day, tried to shake off Eichler by taking advantage of a slip of Bebel's as to date (Bebel had spoken of September instead of October,

1862), as the period of Eichler's Leipzig performance. But trusting
to the effect of this dodge, he was betrayed into the confession
that later on Eichler "made demands upon me for services
he had not rendered me," and that "it was only then that he
remembered that Herr Eichler had been in the service of the
police, and that he had sent him in reports." (See the official verbatim report on the debate on the Anti-Socialist Law, 1878, page
85, published under the title of "Die Sozial-democratie vor dem
deutschen Reichstag."[1]) In other words, the supposed aristocratic lady, or as the Leipzig *Volkstaat* once upon a time drastically put it, "the aristocratic strumpet," turned out to be the
Berlin "Scotland Yard."

About this time—*i.e.*, after Bismarck had prorogued the
Landtag on the 13th October, 1862—Lassalle gave his second
address, "Was nun?"[2] In this he declares that events
have justified the contentions of his first address. The
Kreuz - Zeitung (the organ of the Squirearchy), the War
Minister, Von Roon, and the actual President of the Ministry,
Von Bismarck, had confirmed his theory that constitutional questions are questions of force. Relying upon the force at its disposal, the Government had gone on disregarding the decisions of
the Chamber. It was now less a question of how to assure the
continuance of the Constitution of 1850—in a portion of whose
provisions the people had no interest whatever—than a question
of maintaining the right of the Chamber to vote supplies, and the
making of parliamentary government a reality, for "upon it, and
it *alone*, does the existence of every true constitutional Government
depend." Should they refuse to pay the taxes? No, answers
Lassalle. This is, in itself, an effective weapon only in the hands
of a people which, like the English, has on its side the many
powerful means of organised force. Such a step would only be
wise if it were meant to provoke a general rising. But of this
"it was to be hoped no one, under the *present* circumstances,
would dream." The only way was to say what the actual facts

---

[1] "Social Democracy in the German Reichstag."

[2] "What next?"

were. As soon as the Chamber re-assembled " it must say what the real facts were." This was " the most powerful, political method." The Chamber must make it impossible for the Government to go on governing with mere sham constitutionalism. As soon as the Chamber re-assembled it must, at once, press a vote to the effect that so long as the Government went on violating the Constitution, it would not, by continuing to sit and to legislate, play into the hands of that Government, would not help to maintain the mere semblance of a constitutional state of affairs, and that therefore " it would adjourn for an indefinite period, aye, until the Government gave proof that it would not continue to ignore the vote of the Chamber against supplies." When once the Chamber had passed such a vote, the Government would be beaten. Dissolution would be useless to the Government, since the members would be re-elected on the same lines. But without a Chamber it could not govern. Its credit, its reputation, its influence abroad would be so seriously damaged that sooner or later it would be *forced* to give in. But there was no other way of terminating the conflict. Continuing to sit and refusing to vote other, or, indeed, all Government supplies, would only accustom people and Government to the pleasant habit of disregarding the votes of the Chamber. It would be still worse if the Chamber consented to a compromise possibly as the price for agreeing to the two years military term of service. No ; no surrender in the *constitutional principle* here at stake. The more obstinate the Government proved, the greater would be its humiliation, when it found itself forced to give in. The Government would all the more recognise the social form of the citizen as the superior force, if, after veering round, it had been forced to bow before the people and the Chamber. And, therefore, no " reconciliation-twaddle, gentlemen." No new compromise with the old absolutism, but rather " the hand at the throat, the knee on the breast."

In this address, Lassalle, on the whole, assumes a conciliatory attitude towards the Progressist Party. " For the sake of unity " he will suppress all these serious accusations against them that he has at heart. He only attacks the *Volks Zeitung* and its backers, for their policy of saying that which is *not*. These "poor creatures," in their attempts to "lie" the Government into a constitutional one, were largely responsible for the present condition of things. But " peace to the past, gentlemen ! "

Whether Lassalle really in his heart felt so peaceably inclined, whether he really believed the Progressists would accept his suggestion, or whether all this talk of reconciliation was only rhetorical flourish meant to give him a free hand later on as against the Progressists, is difficult to say. Both may be true. That Lassalle was by no means disinclined to work with the Progressists we have already seen. Many of his personal relations, indeed, must have made such an alliance seem desirable, while from the theoretical standpoint, nothing could, under the circumstances, be advanced against it. On the other hand, however, it had become more and more doubtful whether the Progressists would have anything to do with him, and whether they would allow him to exercise that influence upon their tactics, to which he thought himself entitled.

CHAPTER VI.

MEANTIME, however, the Progressists did not accept the terms of the peace—*i.e.*, the method of fighting recommended by Lassalle. And looking at it from their point of view one cannot blame them. Lassalle's proposition was very good if one was prepared to force things to a head at once, and was in a position to answer a *coup d'état*—and a *coup d'état* was the only resort these tactics left the Government—by a revolution. But the Progressists had not yet progressed so far, and, therefore, preferred the dilatory method. Without a revolution in immediate reserve, the voluntary renunciation of the tribune of the Chamber must end in that notorious "passive resistance" of which Lassalle himself quite rightly made fun. By persistently refusing to vote supplies, one could "say what *is*" quite as loudly and as drastically, could stimulate public opinion as effectively as, or even more effectively than, by means of an indefinite prorogation, which would, into the bargain, give the Government a semblance of right in their violation of the Constitution. But this was the main tactical idea of the Progressists—to make the Government above all else appear as the representative of Might against Right. "Their chief spokesmen," says B. Becker, very justly, "were for the most part men of the juridical and legal profession, accustomed therefore to the law's delays, and inclined to look upon the struggle between the parliamentary majority and the Government as a protracted legal struggle."

And so they again accused Lassalle of placing, like the Government, Might above Right. And now—not as Becker, and after him all the "historians" of the Lassallean movement say, at the time of the first pamphlet on the "Constitution"—Lassalle wrote his essay, "Might and Right," in which he openly threw down the gauntlet to the Progressist Party.

It was easy for him to show in a few words the whole absurdity of this accusation, and to prove to the Progressists to boot that their idol, Schwerin, whose declaration that in Prussia "Right goes before Might," they applauded so loudly, had taken part in a round dozen violations of Right where Might went before Right. "No one in the Prussian State has the right to speak of 'Right!'" he exclaims, "save the Democracy—the old and true Democracy. For it alone has always held to the Right, and has never condescended to any compromise with Might." And : "All *Right* is with the *Democracy alone,* and with it alone *will be Might!*"

This declaration of war, sent in the form of a statement to the Radical Berlin *Reform,* a paper for which Lassalle, so late as June, 1862, had put in a good word with Marx, was refused insertion in its columns, and the *Vossische Zeitung* did the same. The latter also refused to insert the article as a paid advertisement, whereupon Lassalle had it published as an "Open Reply Letter" at Zürich. That the choice of this place for the publication really justified the doubts of the *Vossische Zeitung* "on account of the press laws," did not trouble Lassalle.

Between the publication of the lecture "Was Nun ?" (December, 1862), and the drawing up of the "Open Letter" (February, 1863), two more months passed. But meantime (in January, 1863), the deputation of the Leipzig Central Committee—consisting of the author, Dr. Otto Dammer, and the working-men, F. W. Fritsche and Julius Vahlteich—had been to Berlin to make one last attempt at co-operation with the leaders of the National Association. Nevertheless, they do not seem to have taken this attempt very seriously. They were all three Socialists, and were anxious to get out of the Progressist leaders' own mouths the declaration that they would not hear of an independent working-men's movement, but wanted to keep it in the leading strings of bourgeois Liberalism. And their hopes in this respect were not disappointed. With regard to the question of admission to the National Association, they were given the classical answer, already mentioned, that the workers should consider themselves "honorary members" of the National Association. With regard to the question of the franchise, Unruh, Schulze-Delitzsch, etc., were themselves divided, and, moreover, did not look upon it as a burning one. The three-class electoral system had returned such an excellent Chamber, that surely it might be left alone for a while. That the excellent —*i.e.*, anti-governmental—Chamber was wholly the result of the special conditions of the time never occurred to these gentlemen.

The young Berlin Democrat, and subsequent Progressist member of the Chamber, Ludwig Löwe, directed the attention of the deputation to Ferdinand Lassalle, and, on their return to Leipzig, they entered into communication with him. It is easy to understand how much this must have strengthened his resolve to withdraw his "Peace to the past, gentlemen." When he issued his Open Letter, "Right and Might," it had already been arranged between himself and the Leipzig Committee that the latter were to ask him, in an official communication, to set forth his opinions upon the mission of the working-class movement, and the question of the associations—(*i.e.*, the co-operative societies)—in any form he might think fit, and that this form should be that of a fly-sheet. The Leipzig people—*i.e.*, the active elements in the Working-men's Association—knew perfectly well what they were driving at ; what they were still undetermined about was less the essence of the action to be undertaken than the *programme* of that action. It was by no means "the consciousness of their own want of lucidity," as Bernhard Becker, with his claim to speak truth above everything, says in his "History" of the Lassallean movement—which induced the Leipzig Committee, in an "Appeal to the German Workers," dated 10th February, to declare themselves simultaneously in favour of expediting the summoning of the Workers' Congress, and against over-precipitancy in the matter. The Congress was to be held as soon as possible, but not too soon to prevent Lassalle's answer from first producing its effect. It is only Becker's personal animosity towards Dr.

Otto Dammer that here induces him to falsify history, and to
represent the Committee "as beating a retreat" when nothing
was farther from their thoughts. At the same sitting in which
the appeal just referred to was drawn up, the Committee decided
to write the following letter, which was duly forwarded the next
day, to Lassalle : —

"To Herr Ferdinand Lassalle, in Berlin.

"Most honoured Sir,—Your pamphlet, 'Ueber den beson-
deren Zusammenhang der gegenwärtigen Geschichts-Periode mit
der Idee des Arbeiterstandes' ('On the Special Connection between
the Present Historical Period and the Concept of the Workers'
Estate,') has everywhere here met with great approval from the
workers, and the Central Committee have given expression to this
feeling in the *Arbeiter Zeitung.* On the other hand, very serious
doubts have been expressed in many quarters as to whether the
associations recommended by Schulze-Delitzsch can really benefit
the vast majority of the workers, who possess nothing, and
especially whether they could alter the position of the workers in
the State to the extent that seems necessary. The Central Committee have expressed their views upon this matter in the *Arbeiter
Zeitung* (No. 6) ; they are convinced that co-operative associations cannot, under our present conditions, do enough. But now
the views of Schulze-Delitzsch are being everywhere advocated as
imperative upon the working-class, by which we mean the most
oppressed class of the people, and as no doubt other ways and
means than those proposed by Schulze-Delitzsch might be suggested for attaining the ends of the working-class movement—*i.e.,*
political, material, and intellectual improvement in the condition of the workers—the Central Committee, at its sitting of the
10th February, unanimously resolved :

"'To request you to express your views, in any form you
think fit, upon the working-class movement, and the tactics it
should pursue, and especially upon the value of the associations
for the entirely unpropertied classes of the people.'

"We attach the greatest value to your views as expressed in

the above-mentioned pamphlet, and shall therefore be thoroughly able to appreciate any further communications from yourself. Finally, we would ask you to grant our request as soon as possible, as we are very anxious to push forward the development of the working-class movement.

"With greeting and good wishes on behalf of the Central Committee for summoning a General German Workers' Congress,

"OTTO DAMMER.

"LEIPZIG, 11th Feb., 1863."

The answer to this letter was the "Offene Antwortschreiben an das Zentral-Komitee zur Berufung eines Allgemeinen Deutschen Arbeiter-Kongresses zu Leipzig,"[1] dated the 1st March, 1863.

With this work, and its acceptance by the Committee and by the Leipzig Workingmen's Association itself, begins the actual Socialist agitation of Lassalle, and the history of the "General German Working-men's Association." Lassalle's "Open Reply Letter" begins by controverting the idea that working-men do not need to concern themselves with politics. On the contrary, it is just with politics that they must concern themselves, only they must not do this in such a way as to look upon themselves as the "disinterested choir and sounding-board" of the Progressist Party. The proof that the Progressist Party had no such pretensions is deduced mainly from their conduct during the constitutional struggle, and is, therefore, not always equally convincing. When, *e.g.*, Lassalle on p. 4 of the pamphlet reproaches the Progressist Party for having "made . . . . only . . . . the asserting the right to vote supplies the essence of their struggle," he forgot that in his lecture, "Was Nun?" he had himself defined this as the real and main object of the struggle that must be upheld with the utmost energy. In the same way the Progressist Party might have quoted himself when he counts it a political sin to them that "Their dogma of the supremacy of Prussia forced them to see in the Prussian Government the chosen Messiah of

[1] "Open Reply Letter to the Central Committee for the Summoning of a General German Workers' Congress in Leipzig, by Ferdinand Lassalle."

the new birth of Germany. Yet there is not a single German
Government, including Hesse, that is politically inferior to that of
Prussia, while *there is scarcely a single German Government,* includ-
ing Austria (!!), that is not considerably superior to that of Prussia."[1]

In the main, however, Lassalle was, of course, quite right.
The organisation of the workers, as an independent political party
with a programme of their own, was a historical necessity. If the
development of the political conditions in Germany was such as to
make it seem doubtful whether this was the most propitious
moment for separating the workers from the army of the
Progressist Party, then fighting against absolutism, yet this party
had done enough to challenge such a separation. Moreover, the
independent organisation of the workers did not as yet, in itself,
mean any interference with the aggressive force of the Progressist
Party. That this was actually the result is largely due to the
Progressist Party itself, and to their extremely narrow attitude
towards the new movement. Partly, no doubt, it was also due to
the programme which Lassalle gave to this movement.

In discussing the "Worker's Programme," we saw what an
abstract, purely ideological idea Lassalle combined with the
concept "the State." It is no exaggeration to say that of the
idea of the State he made a veritable cult. "The immemorial
vestal fire of all civilisation, the State, I defend with you against
those modern barbarians" (that is the Manchester Party), he exclaims to the judges of the Berlin *Kammergericht* (Court of Appeal)
in his speech on "Indirect Taxation," and similar passages occur
in almost all his speeches.

The "State" is the weakest point in the Lassallean doctrine;
in the truest sense of the word, its Achilles heel. The old
Hegelian ideological concept of the State induced Lassalle to instil
into the workers a semi-mystical reverence for the State at a time
when, above all, it behoved them to shake off the police State. It
sounds pretty enough when in the "Open Reply Letter" he cries
to the workers: "What, you want to discuss the right of free
migration? I can only answer you with Schiller's distich:

[1] Page 7, 1st Edition.

" ' Jahrelang bedien' ich mich schon meiner Nase zum Riechen,
Aber hab ich an sie auch ein erweisliches Recht ? ' " [1]

Free migration, and the free choice of handicrafts were things
which, in a legislative body, " one dumbly and in silence decrees
but no longer debates." As a matter of fact, however, these
things, like the right of combination, did not even yet exist, while
the workers unquestionably needed them. The true reason why
the questions of free migration and free choice of handicraft had
to be assigned a relatively insignificant position at a working-men's
congress, was because they were also, to a large extent, demands
of middle-class Liberalism. But the discussion of them was not
superfluous, if only because in working-class circles themselves
much confusion as to their meaning still prevailed.

Lassalle pushed these questions on one side, because the demand
for State-help seemed to him more important than they were.
First for its own sake ; but secondly, because he saw in the project
of State-help the only effective means of rousing the working-class
to political action, of at once emancipating them from the yoke of
the bourgeois parties, and of stimulating them to the obtaining of
their democratic demands. And, no doubt, for the time being, the
second reason was the more weighty one to him. It was so also
from the position of affairs themselves. The only question was
whether the method and the means, by which he sought to attain
this end, were the right ones.

To convince the workers of the futility of self-help as
preached by the bourgeoisie, Lassalle adduced the law of wages in
capitalist production as formulated by the classical political
economists, and more especially and most emphatically by
Ricardo. The " iron and inexorable law, according to which, under
the domination of supply and demand, the average wages of labour
remain always reduced to the bare subsistence which, according
to the standard of living of a nation, is necessary for the maintenance of life and the reproduction of the species." If wages periodi-

[1] " For years I have already used my nose for smelling,
But have I really a demonstrable right to that organ ? "

cally rose above this average, the greater number of marriages and births caused an increase of the working-class population, and with it, of the supply of labour, in consequence of which, wages again sank to their former level. If they fell below this average, emigration, greater mortality among the workers, abstinence from marriage, and fewer births, caused a diminution in the supply of labour, in consequence of which wages again went up. Thus " workers and the wages of labour circled for ever round the extreme margin of that which, according to the needs of the time, constitutes the necessary means of subsistence," and this " *never* varies."

Therefore, every attempt of the working-class to improve its condition by the individual efforts of its members, was, of necessity, condemned to failure. It was equally useless to attempt improving the condition of the workers by means of co-operative societies. So long as these were isolated, they might here and there procure the workers certain advantages. But from the moment these societies became general, the workers would, *as producers*, again lose in wages what, *as consumers*, they had gained in the purchase of their goods. Indeed, the condition of the working-class could only be permanently freed from the pressure of this economic law, if the *wages of labour* were replaced by the *possession of the products of labour*, if the working-class became its own employer. But this could not be done by the starting of self-help societies, since these had not the necessary means, and since they were only too often fated to become permeated by the employer-spirit, and its members to be transformed into the " repulsive caricature of working-men with working-men's means, and employers' minds." Great problems could only be solved by great means, and, therefore, societies must be started on a vast scale, and must be extended to the factories of modern industry, but the means to do this—the necessary capital, *i.e.*, the necessary credit—must be provided by the *State*.

This was certainly in no way Communism or Socialism. " Nothing could be further removed from so-called Communism or Socialism than this demand which would allow the working-classes to retain just as to-day *their individual freedom, their individual mode of life,* and the *individual reward of labour*," and to stand in no other relation to the State, than that through its agency the required capital, *i.e.,* the credit necessary for their societies, would be obtained. Now the true function of the State was to facilitate and help on the great forward march of mankind. " For this the *State exists,* for this it has *always* served, and must *serve.*" But " what then is the State ?" And Lassalle cites the figures of the Prussian statistics of incomes for the year 1851, according to which in that year 89 per cent. of the population had had an income of less than 200 thalers, and $7\frac{1}{4}$ per cent. of the population an income of from 200 to 400 thalers, so that, therefore, $96\frac{1}{4}$ per cent. of the population were in a miserable, oppressed condition. " *To them,* then, gentlemen, to the suffering classes does the State *belong,* not to us, to the upper classes, for of them it is composed! What is the State ? I asked, and now you see from a few figures, more easily than you could from big volumes, the answer: *Yours,* the poorer classes' great association,—that is the State." And how to obtain this intervention from the State ? This would be possible only by means of universal and direct suffrage. Only when the legislative bodies of Germany were returned by universal and direct suffrage, " then, and then *only,* will you be able to induce the State to undertake this its duty." Universal and direct suffrage . . . " is not only your political, it is also your social fundamental principle, the fundamental condition of all social help." Therefore let the workers organise for a universal German Working-men's Association, whose object should be the introduction into all German countries of universal and direct suffrage. If this demand were taken up by the 89 to 96 per cent. of the population as a *question of the belly,* and therefore distributed with the warmth of the belly throughout the whole of the national body, there was no power on earth that could withstand it long. " The whole art of *practical* success lies in this : in the concentration of all power, at all times, upon one single point—upon the most important point, and in turning neither to the right nor to the left. Don't look either to the right or to the left, be deaf to all that is not

called universal and direct suffrage, or is related thereto, and
may lead to it."

This, roughly speaking, is the informing idea of the "Open
Reply Letter," and, at the same time, of the whole Lassallean
agitation. For though, of course, this does not represent the
whole of Lassalle's aims, nevertheless, to the very end Lassalle
held fast to limiting the movement to this one point : " Universal
suffrage in order to obtain State help for productive co-operative
societies," and this on the principle stated above, that the
art of practical success consists in concentrating all forces, at all
times, upon one single point. It is important to keep this in
mind, for those who wish to estimate rightly Lassalle's labours as
an agitator. These labours, in the beginning at least, had been
directed towards obtaining an immediate practical result. In the
" Open Reply Letter " Lassalle specially refers to the agitation
and success of the Anti-Corn Law League in England, and it
would seem that he had the English Chartist agitation in his
mind also. This is proved by the sentence about the "question
of the belly," which recalls the declaration of the Chartist
preacher, Stephens : "Chartism, my friends, is not a political
question, but a fork and knife question."

If we now ask ourselves whether an immediate practical success
was actually possible for the agitation thus planned out, under
the then existing conditions, I believe I may unhesitatingly
answer in the affirmative. That Bismarck later on—it is true
only for the North German Reichstag—actually introduced universal suffrage, does not, it seems to me, affect the question. All
kinds of circumstances might have prevented this, without altering the fact that Lassalle's calculation was, for the time, a right
one. On the contrary. Although the three-class electoral system
was retained for the Prussian Landtag, Lassalle's calculation was,
all the same, right; it was quite in keeping with the existing
political situation. Lassalle knew perfectly well that if in the
Progressist camp universal suffrage had many enemies, and, on
the whole, only lukewarm friends, the governmental circles, on
the contrary, looked more and more askant at the three-class

electoral system. The governmental papers spoke quite openly in this sense, and, moreover, as we have seen, Lassalle had plenty of connections to keep him well informed as to which way the wind blew in court and official circles. If the Government would not give way on the constitutional struggle, it could, unless a foreign war came about—and that also might prove fatal—do nothing but emulate Napoleon III. : dissolve the Landtag and introduce another more "democratic" suffrage. And the Government was the more driven to such a step that a strong movement independent of the Progressists was growing up, which had inscribed upon its banner the abolition of the three-class electoral system. Especially, in view of a possible war, this must have seemed to the Government the best way to escape having a whole nation as an enemy attacking them in the rear.[1]

[1] We have already, whilst considering his " Italian War," seen with what coolness—quite inconsistent with the *rôle* of "good patriot "— Lassalle regarded the reaction of external complications upon internal politics. Very characteristic of this attitude is a passage in his pamphlet "Was Nun?" This passage should be quoted here because the proposition there set forth by Lassalle, practically admits of only two solutions ; either a *coup d'état* or a revolution. Thereupon Lassalle, to show how impossible and untenable would be the foreign diplomatic position of the Prussian Government if his proposition were accepted, proceeds :

" Let none of you, gentlemen, imagine this is an unpatriotic argument. The politician, like the naturalist, must, once for all, consider all that is, and must, therefore, take into consideration *all* active forces. The antagonism of States, their differences, their jealousies, their diplomatic conflicts, *are* an active force, and whether for good or for ill must, therefore, be reckoned with. And in addition to this, gentlemen, how often, in the stillness of my chamber, busied with historical studies, have I had occasion to completely realise the great truth—that it is almost impossible for us to conceive in what a condition of barbarism we, and the world generally, would still be plunged, were it not that the jealousy and antagonism of governments have since all time been an effective means for forcing a government to progress internally. But finally, gentlemen, the existence of the German people is not of so precarious a nature that a defeat of their governments would constitute a real menace for the existence of the nation. If, gentlemen, you study history carefully, and with true insight, you will see that the strides in civilisation achieved by our

From the point of view of immediate, practical success, Lassalle
was, then, undoubtedly right.   It was possible to obtain universal
suffrage in the way worked out by him.   Truly for a price.
If the Government granted it to avoid being obliged to give
in to the Progressist Party, the solution of the constitutional
struggle would be, at least, still further postponed.   " Be deaf to
all that is not called universal and direct suffrage, or is related
thereto, and may lead to it," he says in the " Open Reply Letter."
Universal suffrage once obtained, it would also—at least, one is
logically bound to assume this as self-understood in Lassalle,
although he does not expressly say so—solve this question.   But
was Lassalle's expectation in respect to universal suffrage, as well
as the expectations which he based upon this, justified by actual
facts ?

The only experience obtainable in Lassalle's time with regard
to universal and direct suffrage, was furnished by France.   And
here the results were not particularly in its favour.   During

people, are so gigantic and powerful, have been such a guidance and
exemplar for the rest of Europe, that there can be absolutely no question
of the necessity for and indestructibility of our national existence.   So that
should we be involved in a great foreign war, it is possible that our individual governments, the Saxon, Prussian, Bavarian, might break down
under it, but Phœnix-like there would arise from their ashes, indestructible, that which alone can concern *us—the German people !* "   (" Was
Nun ? " 1st Ed., pp. 33-34.)

These lines contain much that is true, but two facts must not be lost
sight of.   First, that important a factor in the progress of nations as the
rivalry of governments may have, and undoubtedly has been, it has very
frequently acted in the opposite direction, and has proved an obstacle to
progress.   We have only to call to mind the two phases of the militarism
of to-day.   Secondly, although a foreign war would not remove a great
civilised people from the ranks of the nations, yet it might so seriously
affect them in their vital interests, that war is a contingency we may take
into consideration, but should not speculate upon.   In the passage quoted,
Lassalle only does the former, but as its concluding sentence, and his
letters show, he was not disinclined towards the latter course also—a not
uncommon habit, by the way, but not on that account the less reprehensible.

the February Republic, universal suffrage had certainly sent a number of Socialists to the National Assembly, but the voice of these Socialists had been drowned by that of the representatives of the different bourgeois parties, and universal suffrage had so little prevented Bonaparte's *coup d'état*, that, on the contrary, Bonaparte had been able to make the *coup d'état* as the " champion of universal suffrage." And moreover, the February Republic, when it came into existence, was hailed by the Parisian proletariat as the *social* Republic. Its proclamation had been preceded by a period of immense Socialist propaganda on a very large scale, and so warranted the assumption that this Republic might have become in course of time a really Socialistic Republic. Why didn't it come about? Why, rather, was it overthrown by the Empire?

When Lassalle at the end of the " Worker's Programme," says that what was overthrown on the 2nd December, 1851, was " not *the* Republic," but the bourgeois Republic, which, by the electoral Law of May, 1850, had abolished universal suffrage, and had introduced what amounted to a property qualification in order to exclude the workers ; when he says that the Republic of universal suffrage would " have found in the breasts of the French workers an insurmountable barrier," he is simply echoing one of the cries of the small middle - class Revolutionists, *à la* Ledru Rollin, which does not answer the question, but only evades it. Where was this " insurmountable barrier," when the Chamber, elected on the basis of universal suffrage, repealed that suffrage? Why did not the Parisian workers prevent this " *coup d'état* of the bourgeoisie "? If Lassalle had asked himself this question he would have found that the February Republic could not endure as a social Republic, because the class upon which it would as such have had to rely, was not yet sufficiently developed—*i.e.*, not sufficiently developed in the *social* sense of the word. The modern industrial proletariat was there ; it had even been strong enough for one moment to overthrow the whole existing order of things, but not strong enough to keep it down. Here we again see the fundamental fallacy of the Lassallean method of thought. Even when he tries to enter into the deeper causes of historical events, his juridical bent of mind prevents his really getting to the bottom of the social side of these, and even when he deals with their economic side he does so when this has already —if I may so express myself—crystallised in the juridical form. This alone can explain why Lassalle, to show the workers of what elements the population of the State is composed, confined himself, and that *exclusively*, to the statistics of *incomes*. The dispute, which arose out of this passage in the " Open Reply Letter," is comparatively unimportant. Whether Lassalle's percentages were slightly inaccurate in this direction or in that, at bottom matters very little. The fact that the great mass of the population lives in poverty, while only a small minority riots in superfluity, this the Wackernagles and his fellows, who at this time opposed Lassalle, could not, with all their pettifogging arguments, argue out of the world. It is far more important that Lassalle completely ignored what different elements composed that 96 or 89 per cent. of the population, whose "great association" he called the State. Nor does he at all note how great a proportion of these were small artisans, and small peasants, and, above all, agricultural labourers, a section of whom were still absolutely under the spiritual control of their employers. Over half the population of Prussia was at this time agricultural ; the larger towns did not play any thing like the part they do to-day, and, from the standpoint of industrial development, the whole eastern portion of the kingdom was only a desert with isolated oases.[1]

Under such conditions, what difference could universal suffrage make in the composition of the Chamber ? Was a better result to be expected from it than from universal suffrage in the France of 1848 and 1849 ? Surely not. It might send a certain number of labour representatives to Parliament, and this, in itself, was

---

[1] While 3,428,457 persons were employed in agriculture in Prussia at this time, only 766,180 were employed in factory industries, including the business managers and clerks.

certainly desirable. But for the rest it was bound to debase the composition of the Chamber instead of improving it, and this, the more fully it realised what Lassalle expected—*i.e.*, returned a legislative body that should be "the true and faithful image of the people that had elected it." ("Worker's Programme.") For miserable as the Chamber then was, yet it was at least bourgeois-liberal. Lassalle forgot that the indigent classes, although they may under certain circumstances collectively supply revolutionary troops, are by no means wholly and solely revolutionary classes ; he forgot that of the 89 per cent., only a portion as yet consisted of modern proletarians.

If, therefore, it was possible to obtain universal suffrage, it by no means followed that this would bring about, within a measurable time, that which universal suffrage itself again was to be a means of obtaining. Considering the degree of education, political and otherwise, of the great mass of the population, the immediate effect of the suffrage might have been the very opposite. Instead of sending representatives of modern principles to the Chamber, it might have increased the number of representatives of retrogression. Not all Progressists were the opponents, or luke-warm friends of universal suffrage from class-interest. There were among them a large proportion of ideologists, whom the development of events in France had rendered sceptical as to its value. Socialists also thought thus. We need but refer to Rodbertus, who, in his "Open Letter" to the Leipzig Committee, also points to France as an example that universal suffrage "does not of necessity give the power of the State into the hands of the working-class." It had been said, he goes on, that universal suffrage was to be only a means towards the end, but means "may be used for different ends, and occasionally for the most opposite ones." "Are you," he asks, "certain that here the means must of absolute necessity lead to the ends desired by you ? I do not think this." From Lassalle's letters to Rodbertus it also appears that Rodbertus's reason for refusing to join the General German Workers' Association, in spite of Lassalle's urgent importunities, was almost more due to his opposition to universal suffrage than to his hostile opinion as to the value of the productive associations.[1]

And whatever else one may think of Rodbertus, his motives are unmistakably set forth in the concluding sentences of his letter. He there advises the workers—although Lassalle was right to say such questions were no longer to be discussed—to place the demand for free migration and free choice of calling in their programme as self-understood, in order to warn off as effectually as possible any reactionary who might harm them.

If Rodbertus and others exaggerated the danger of Bonapartism, Lassalle on his side certainly made too light of it. The way in which he actually did, later on, veer round in this direction, was, from the outset, to be expected with his method of reasoning. In this connection a passage in Lassalle's letter to Marx—from which I have already partly quoted—of the 20th June, 1859, that deals with the Italian war, is very characteristic. Lassalle writes :

" In the beginning, when the national cry for war against France broke out, and was taken up so passionately everywhere, the *Volks Zeitung* (Bernstein, in my opinion an arch-reactionary, is its editor) exclaimed triumphantly in a leading article : ' Would you know what this outcry of all the peoples against France means ? Would you understand its world-wide historical import ? The *emancipation* of Germany from the *political development of France*—that is what it signifies.' Need I explain in detail to you the ultra-reactionary meaning of this shriek of triumph ? Surely not ! A *popular* war against France—and our petty bourgeois democrats, our decentralists, the *enemies of all*

---

[1] Originally Rodbertus had said in his " Open Letter " : " And I *repeat* that from the productive associations also I expect absolutely nothing, as a contribution to what is called the solution of the social question." At Lassalle's request these words were, however, omitted in print, as in matter they were a repetition of what had already been said in the letter, while in this drastic form they necessarily " must discourage the workers, if they saw such marked differences between the leaders." (Letter of Lassalle to Rodbertus, August 22nd, 1863.)

social advance, gain, for a long, long time, an incalculable increase of power. Even when we are well into the German Revolution, the effect of this tendency would make itself felt. Assuredly we do not need to infuse new strength into this the most dangerous enemy we have—*i.e.*, the German petty-bourgeois individualism, by a bloody antagonism to the Romance - social spirit in its classical form in France."

Thus Lassalle. The editor of the *Volks Zeitung,* now dead, unquestionably deserved the title Lassalle gives him, in many respects : but least of all, perhaps, on account of the passage quoted by Lassalle. The political development of France was, at that time, Bonapartism, while the party of the *Volks Zeitung* swore by England as its political model. This was, certainly, very one-sided, but still not reactionary, or only reactionary in as much as it was one-sided. But Lassalle's conception, which saw in the State centralisation of France a product of the " Romance-social " spirit, and identified this with the fundamental idea of Socialism, whilst entirely overlooking its reactionary side, was not less one-sided.

So much for the political side of the Lassallean programme] Let us now consider its economic side.

CHAPTER VII.

THE "OPEN REPLY LETTER"; ITS ECONOMIC PORTION.—THE IRON LAW OF WAGES, AND PRODUCTIVE CO-OPERATIVE SOCIETIES WITH STATE-HELP.

THE law of wages upon which Lassalle based his theory, and to which he added the name "iron," corresponds—as I think I have demonstrated elsewhere[1]—with a particular method of production —small industry—and a condition of society resulting from it, and has, therefore, at least been outlived in the society of modern industry, with its increased facilities of communication, its accelerated cycle of crises, stagnation, and prosperity, its rapid advance in the productivity of labour, etc. Moreover, this theory presupposes an absolutely free movement of supply and demand on the labour market. But this movement is at once interfered with as soon as the working-class, as an organised body, faces the employers, or as soon as the State, by its legislation, interferes with the regulation of the conditions of labour. So that when the Liberals replied to Lassalle that his law of wages no longer held good, that it was antiquated, they were to some extent justified. But only to some extent. For these good people, in their turn, fell into far graver errors than Lassalle.

Lassalle laid special stress upon the "iron" character of the laws determining wages, because he believed he was dealing the deadliest blow at modern Society by proving that the worker never, under any circumstances, received the full product of his labour, his full share of the commodity produced by him. He gave the question a legal character, which, from the propagandist point of view, proved extremely effective. But he himself by no means went to the heart of the question. Even under earlier

---

[1] See *Neue Zeit:* 1890-91 : " The Iron Law of Wages."

forms of production the worker did not get the full results of his labour; and if an "iron" law prevents wages from permanently falling below a given minimum, and if this minimum itself rises—as Lassalle expressly admitted—in the course of development, rises slowly, it is true, but still rises, it became difficult to give proofs of the actual necessity for the intervention of the State.

The really material question at issue was not raised by Lassalle until later on, and then only incidentally. The position of the working-class in modern Society is so unbearable, and compares so unfavourably with every former method of production, not because the worker receives only a fraction of the new value produced by him, but because this fractional payment is combined with the *uncertainty* of his proletarian existence ; because of the dependence of the workers upon the contractions of the world-market following one another in ever shorter periods of time, on constant revolutions of industry, and altered conditions of distribution ; because of the crying contrast between the character of production, ever becoming more socialised, and its anarchical distribution ; and with all this the growing impossibility for the individual workers to free themselves from the double dependence upon the employing class, and the vicissitudes of the industrial cycle ; because of the constant threat of being thrown from one sphere of industry into another lower one, or into the army of unemployed. The dependence of the worker has only become greater with his apparent freedom. It is this which, with iron weight, presses upon the working-class, and its pressure grows with the growing development of Capitalism. The rate of wages, on the other hand, varies to-day with the various branches of industry, from literally starvation wages to wages which represent a certain amount of comfort. In the same way the amount of exploitation in the different industries also varies considerably, in certain cases wages being higher, in others lower, than in the earlier epochs of production. Both depend upon very variable factors ; both differ, not only from industry to industry, but are in each of these subject to the greatest changes. The only thing constant is the tendency of capital to raise the

rate of exploitation, to squeeze surplus-labour in one way or another out of the worker.

The chief fault of Lassalle's proposed remedy lay, from the
very outset, in his representing as the essential cause of the misery
of the working-class in the Society of to-day, that which is certainly not the characteristic feature of the modern method of
production—for, as we have said, the worker has at no time
received the full results of his labour.   He ignores, or to be just
to Lassalle, he underrates the strength and extent of the laws of
the production of commodities, and their economic and social
re-action upon modern economic life as a whole.   Here again we
must carefully distinguish between Lassalle's means and Lassalle's
end.   His end was, of course, to abolish the present production of
commodities ; but his means left it untouched.   His end was
organised, social production; his means were individual association,
which so far only differed from the Schulze plan in that it was to
be brought about by means of State-credit and State-help.   Everything else, the fusion of the associations, etc., was left to their
own voluntary decisions.   It was *expected* of them, but was not
made a condition.   The State was to advance the necessary means,
by guaranteeing credit, but only to such workmen as desired to
start associations.

The associations in any given industry, so long as they did not
embrace the whole of that industry, would, therefore, have to
compete with establishments of the same kind already in existence,
and would thus be forced to submit to the conditions of such
competition.   The inevitable consequence of this must be that,
within the associations themselves, differences of interest would
arise ; that every association would have to try and force up its
own profits as high as possible, even though it were at the expense
of other associations, or of other categories of labour.   With or
without State-credit, the associations remained private concerns,
made up of more or less large groups of workers.   Individual
qualities, individual advantages, individual good fortune, played a
conspicuous part in them ; the question of profit and loss had the
same significance for them as for other private business concerns,

Lassalle certainly believed, first of all—judging from the eagerness with which productive co-operative associations had been taken up in Paris in 1848—that at least *all* the workers engaged in certain industries in particular localities, would immediately unite to form one great association in each such place. Secondly, he distinctly declared later on in his " Bastiat-Schulze," that in each town the State would have to allow *only one* association in every particular trade the benefit of State-credit, leaving all workers of that trade free to enter into such an association. (See " Herr Bastiat-Schulze," p. 217, 1st Ed.) But even such locally homogeneously-organised associations would still remain nationally competitive. The economic consequences of this national competition were to be further neutralised by great insurance and credit unions of the associations amongst themselves. It is obvious, however, that this insurance society was a chimera, unless it was simply another name for a national organisation, and for a national monopoly of industry. Otherwise over-production would very soon break up the insurance association. And over-production was unavoidable if the State, as required by Lassalle, kept the entrance to these associations " open " to *all* workers of the same trade. Here Lassalle, pricked on by his Socialist conscience, involves himself in a great contradiction. " To keep the entrance into the association open," was to bind the association to admit every worker who applied for admission. But, according to the " Open Reply Letter," the association was to be entirely independent, *vis-à-vis* of the State, only giving the latter the right of approving the rules, and of looking after the business management in order to safeguard its own interests. But under the arrangement set forth above, the association was, on the contrary, transformed from an independent into a public—*i.e.*, under existing conditions—into a State institute —an internal contradiction, on which it must inevitably be wrecked.

And yet another contradiction in the Lassallean productive associations. So long as the associations included only a fraction of those belonging to any given branch of industry, they were subject to the compulsory laws of competition, and this the more as Lassalle had in his eye that working of production on a great factory-like scale, which makes the great industries of the world-market. But wherever there is competition there is also commercial risk ; competition forces the concern, whether managed by an individual, a joint stock company, or an association, to take its chance of its goods being at any time thrown on the market as below value—*i.e.*, as products of not socially necessary labour. Competition and over-production, competition and stagnation, competition and bankruptcy, are, in the Society of to-day, inseparable. Command of production by the producers themselves is only possible in proportion as competition is done away with among them, is only attainable by means of monopoly. But while, in our Society of to-day, competition has the important mission of protecting the consumers against fraud, and constantly reducing the costs of production, monopoly, on the contrary, tends to defraud the consumers for the benefit of the monopolists, and to hamper, where it does not altogether arrest, the development of technical skill. And the latter is especially the case where the workers concerned are themselves the monopolists. The getting rid of their commercial risk for the associations, must, therefore, within the framework of our capitalist society, necessarily be brought about—if, indeed, it could be brought about at all—at the expense of the consumers, who, in any case, represent, as compared with the producers, the vast majority.

In a Socialist community it would, of course, be easy to prevent this. But such a community will not proceed to the socialisation of production by way of subventioned productive co-operative societies, but will, even though the co-operative form should be made use of, start with organising production on a socialised basis. Transplanted into the midst of a capitalist society however, co-operation must, in one way or another, always assume a capitalistic character. The Lassallean co-operative societies would only have differed from those of Schulze-Delitzsch quantitatively, not qualitatively ; only in extent, not in essence.

Such also was the opinion of Rodbertus, who was far too accomplished an economist to overlook this weak side of the

Lassallean co-operative societies. We have seen from the letter of Lassalle to Rodbertus, already quoted, how sharply Rodbertus had intended criticising these in his "Open Letter," and the subsequent letters of Lassalle to Rodbertus show us clearly enough what had been the latter's chief objection. But this is shown even more clearly in the letters of Rodbertus to Rudolph Meyer, and it may not be without interest to quote some of the passages referred to here.

On the 6th September, 1871, Rodbertus writes :

". . . . In addition to this it is also demonstrable that that collective property which the Social Democrats are to-day striving for—that of agrarian communities and productive co-operative associations—is a far worse form of landed and capitalist property, leading to far greater injustice than the present *individualist* form. In this the workers are still following Lassalle. In my letters I had, however, convinced him of the absurdities and injustice which must result from such a form of property, and (what especially annoyed him) that he was not the creator of this idea at all, but had borrowed it from Proudhon's ' Idée Generale de la Révolution.' "[1]

Letter of May 24th, 1872 :

" I have yet a third reason, of a general nature, to urge against this mode of payment. [He is referring to the sharing of business profits.] It must remain either a bonus, as Settegast rightly says—and the social question will not be solved by means of ' tips '—or it must develop into a claim to participate in the management of the concern, and with this finally into collective property in the individual funds of the concern. But this col-

---

[1] Proudhon himself had " borrowed " his productive associations from Louis Blanc, or, more correctly, had botched up Louis Blanc's association-plan in his own way. Lassalle's proposition comes midway between those of Louis Blanc and of Proudhon ; in common with the former, he asks for State aid, and with the latter the independence of the associations.

lective property does not move along the lines of social development.   The proof of this would take me too far afield, but still I
had already forced Lassalle so far in our correspondence that he
wrote to me in one of his last letters : ' But who tells you, then,
that I want the funds for carrying on the concern to *belong* to the
productive association ? ' [*sic !*]   And, indeed, it can't be done !
The collective property of the *workers,* in the individual concerns,
would be a far worse kind of property than the individualist property in land and capital, or even than the property of a capitalist
association. . . ."

Such a passage as is here quoted, appears in none of the
hitherto published letters of Lassalle to Rodbertus.   But it is
hardly to be supposed that Rodbertus would have spoken so
positively unless he had had the actual text before him.   Probably he later on mislaid this letter.   Moreover, there is no valid
reason against Lassalle's having, in fact, once expressed himself
in this way.   In all Lassalle's speeches it is rather of the interest
which the associations are to pay the State on the capital advanced
that he speaks.   Thus, in this sentence there is not even a concession to the standpoint of Rodbertus.   But, on the other hand,
we do find such a concession, and so strong a one that it is tanta-
mount to a condemnation—unconsciously—of the productive
associations in Lassalle's letter to Rodbertus on the 26th May,
1863.   He there says :

"But, on the other hand, it is clear as daylight that when the
land, capital, and the products of labour belong to the worker,[1]
there can be no question of a solution of the social problem.   The
same result will, therefore, be approximately attained also when
land and capital are provided for the worker's use, and the product of labour belongs to him.   In the agricultural associations

---

[1] In Professor Ad. Wagner's edition of Lassalle's letters the passage
reads "does *not* belong."   The "not," however, as the subsequent text
shows, is a printer's error.   Nor does it appear in Rudolph Meyer's reproduction of the letter.   (See loc. cit., p. 463.)

the worker will then get either *more* or *less* than the product of his labour. In industrial associations he will, as a rule, get more than the results of his labour. I know all this perfectly, and when I write my economic work, shall demonstrate it very explicitly."

In the next letter, either because Rodbertus had not thoroughly grasped the import of the above passage, or because he wanted to force Lassalle into a corner, Lassalle declares himself still more definitely. He writes [I omit a parenthesis of no importance here] : " My statement : ' In agricultural associations the worker will then get either *more* or *less* than the product of his labour,' is surely easy enough to understand so far as the ' more' is concerned. I can't in the least understand any difficulty arising with regard to this passage.

" The associations in the more favourable or better situated lands, would, in the first instance, get exactly the same rent of land as the individual owner of them does now. And consequently get *more* than their actual produce, the actual product of labour.

" But from this fact alone, that an individual in Society gets *more* than his legitimate product of labour, it follows that another must get *less* than with a legitimate division of the product of labour—as we both understand this (see the end of your third Social Letter)—he would receive as the reward of his labour.

" More accurately : What is the fair product of my labour (in the sense of the final solution of the social question, therefore, in the sense of the ' idea' which I here always assume as the criterion and measure of comparison in the ' more or less ') ? Is it the agricultural or industrial product which I individually can, under certain given conditions, produce, while another, under more advantageous conditions, can, with the same amount of labour, produce more, and a third, under more unfavourable conditions, with the same amount of labour, produce less ? Surely not ! *My* product of labour would be the *share* in the common socialised productions, which is determined by the *relations* in

which *my* quantum of labour stands to the quantum of labour of
the whole of Society.

"After the conclusion of your third Social Letter, *you* cannot
possibly dispute this.

"And consequently, so long as the workers of the one association receive rent of land, the workers of the other associations
that are not in this position, get *less* than their due share, less
than the legitimate product of their labour."

Thus far, Lassalle. A misunderstanding is here no longer
possible. The "idea" which Lassalle assumes in his "more or
less," is the Communist idea, which takes the total social product of labour, and not the product of labour of an individual or
a group. Lassalle was perfectly conscious of this : that so long as
the latter forms the standard of comparison, a portion of the
population will receive more, another necessarily less than under
a fair division should come to it as its share of the common
socialised labour ;—*i.e.*, that, in the first instance, the associations
would create a *new inequality.* And for this very reason he had,
as Lassalle declares again and again, carefully avoided the words,
"solution of the social question"—in the working out of his proposal, "not from any practical timidity and diffidence, but on these
theoretical grounds."

In the course of his letter, Lassalle explains that the inequality
between agricultural co-operative associations could easily be
overcome by a graduated land tax, which is to "abolish all
rents of land, *i.e.*, placing them in the hands of the State, and
leaving the workers only the actually equalised results of their
labours"—rents of land in the Ricardian sense.[1] The land tax
would provide for the payment for the handing over of the soil to
the associated workers, and—as Lassalle expresses it—" even from
justice or envy, would be warmly supported " by the agricultural associations. But this rent of land would "supply the

---

[1] *i.e.*, as the excess of the product of the land, above a certain minimum
amount, below which, indeed, the land is not cultivated, because it does
not even yield an equivalent for the labour put into it.

State with means for defraying the costs of education, science, art, and public expenditure of all kinds." In the industrial associations, on the other hand, equalisation was to be brought about by the associations of every single branch of trade, as soon as they were combined in one great association, abandoning all private middle-man business, all sales being carried on in sale-rooms provided by the State. "Would not this at the same time make an end of what to-day men call over-production and industrial crises ? "

The idea of State-ownership or the socialisation of rents of land [1] is a thoroughly rational one—*i.e.*, contains no intrinsic contradiction. And in my opinion it is extremely probable, that at a certain stage of development it will, in some way, be realised. The idea of uniting into one body the associations is, on the contrary, only a pious hope, which *may* be brought about, but need not necessarily be accomplished so long as participation in it is left to the good pleasure of the individual associations. And even should this be accomplished, this would by no means prevent members of the individual associations from receiving in their share of the proceeds of them a larger, or under certain conditions, a smaller quota of the common socialised product, than would be due to them on the basis of the totality of labour expended. There would still be the interests of the associations as against the social interests.

Let us listen once more to Rodbertus.

In a letter to Rudolph Meyer of the 16th August, 1872, he refers to an article in the *Neue Sozial Democrat*,[2] which maintained that Lassalle had belonged to the "most advanced tendency of Socialism," and thinks this is probably true, but "it is just as true that Lassalle, and the (*New*) *Sozial Democrat* originally had striven for a productive co-operative association like that which Schulze-Delitzsch wanted, that is, one in which the pro-

---

[1] Not to be confounded with the suggestions of Henry George, Flür-scheim, etc., since Lassalle *assumes* the universal existence of the associations, without which, as we have seen earlier, every reform of taxation must, in his opinion, be wrecked by the iron law of wages.

[2] The *New Social Democrat*.

fits of capital were to belong to the workers themselves, only that Schulze-Delitzsch wanted them to save the capital for this purpose themselves, and Lassalle wanted the State—our present State, too—to provide it for them (whether as gift or loan, is perhaps not quite clear). But a productive association, which pockets the profits of capital, assumes capitalist *property*, and ownership. How then is it possible to reconcile that most advanced tendency with such an association?"

Rodbertus now considers the question whether the productive association could be regarded as a "provisional institution," and after a few remarks of a general nature, continues : "Enough, the productive association which Lassalle and the *Sozial Democrat* really did strive for, cannot even serve as a transition stage towards those 'most advanced' aims, for, given human nature, it would not lead to universal brotherhood, but would take us back to the most acute form of corporate property, in which only the persons of the possessors were changed, and that would prove a thousand times more hateful than the individualist property of to-day. The transition from this to universal State property can never be by means of guild or collective property (they come much to the same thing) ; rather, it is exactly this individual property which is the transition from co-operative property to State property. And in this lies the confusion of the Social Democrats (and in it lay Lassalle's) : *i.e.*, that along with this *most advanced aim* (which, with Lassalle, too, was not yet to excite any *practical* interest), productive association is to be attained by means of capitalist profits, and therefore, capitalist property. Never, then, has the cart been put before the horse so thoroughly as by the Berlin Social Democrats (and their leader, Lassalle, also, in as much as he, too, strove after this 'most advanced aim') and *Marx knows this very well.*" (Letters, etc., of Rodbertus-Jagetzow. I., 226 et. seq.)

I have quoted Rodbertus so fully because his was the most objective attitude assumed towards Lassalle, because his conception of the State had much in common with Lassalle's, and because no one probably discussed the productive associations with Lassalle so thoroughly as he did. Certainly his judgment is not altogether unbiased either, for it is notorious that he had a theory of his own on the solution of the "social question"—*i.e.*, the working normal *work* day (fixed not only by time but by the amount of work done), and wages of labour in proportion. But in the main matter he places his finger quite rightly on the weak point in the Lassallean association when he says that it puts the cart before the horse. Lassalle desired the socialisation of production, and of the means of production, and because he thought the time not come for saying so already to the "mob"—by which he meant the rabble of idealess persons of *all* parties—and yet wished to disseminate the idea itself among the masses, he set forth what seemed to him a less dangerous postulate of productive co-operative associations with State-credit.

In this he committed the same mistake which, in his essay on " Franz von Sickingen," he represented as the tragic fault of Sickingen. As that essay puts it, he " juggled " with the " idea," and deceived his friends more than his enemies. But, like Sickingen, he did so in good faith. Though Lassalle repeatedly assured Rodbertus that he was ready to give up the associations as soon as the latter would show him an equally easy and effective means to the same ends, we should not conclude from this that Lassalle was not thoroughly convinced of the excellence of his own means. Everyone makes such declarations, and the greater his faith in his own cause, the more readily will he make them. And how much this was the case with Lassalle is shown by his last remarks on the associations in answering Rodbertus : " In short, I can't understand how anyone can fail to see that the association, proceeding from the *State*, is the organic germ of development that will lead on to all that lies beyond." He must, then, be entirely acquitted of the reproach of having, in this demand, recommended to the workers something of whose justice he was not convinced, a reproach that would be far more serious than the making of a theoretical blunder.

Lassalle believed that in the means of co-operative associations with State-credit, means that were to serve the final end—*i.e.*, the

realisation of a Socialist society—all the chief essentials of that
aim were already contained ; and that here, in fact—and upon
this he lays such great stress—" the means themselves are absolutely imbued with the very nature of the end." Now, certainly,
co-operation in a small way is, of course, a partial realisation of
the Socialist principle of Communism, and the demand for State-
help is an application of the idea for using the State machinery as
a means towards the economic emancipation of the working-
class, while it is also a means of possibly maintaining the connection of this with the question as a whole—a connection that
was lost in the associations of the Schulze type.   So far,
we not only cannot reproach Lassalle, but must warmly acknowledge the unity of his conception.   We have seen what his
conception of the State was, how for him the State was not the
existing political expression of a particular social condition, but
the realisation of an ethical concept, the eternal " truth " of whose
nature might be modified by existing historical influences, but
could not be subverted.   Holding such a view, it is, however, only
logical to see in the demand for State-help something more than
a mere practical measure, and as Lassalle did, to ascribe to it as a
fundamental principle of Socialism the significance of an independent principle.[1]

  And in the same way, the demand for productive co-operative
societies stands in the closest intellectual relation to Lassalle's
theory of the iron law of wages.   It is based upon the same
economic hypotheses.   In a word, I should say that everything
here is cast in the same mould.

  But that Lassalle believed in the rightness of his means does
not justify him in expressing himself as vaguely as possible as to
his aims.   He who, in the already quoted essay on " Franz von

  [1] So, too, holding this view, it was only logical for Lassalle, in his Leipzig speech on " The Working-Class Question," *e.g.*, to blame the so-called
Manchester men among other things, because if they could, they " would
allow the State to be submerged in Society."   As a matter of fact, however, the really characteristic point is that the Manchester men would like
the State to be submerged in *Capitalist* Society.

Sickingen," had so admirably demonstrated the danger that lurks
"in concealing the true and final aim of the movement from
others (and often, therefore, even from oneself);" he who had
seen in this concealment of Sickingen his "moral crime" that
must lead inevitably to his destruction, the result of a want of
confidence in the strength of the ideas he represented, a "devia-
tion from his own principle," a "half defeat,"—he should have
been the last to direct the movement towards a means, instead of
to its actual end. The excuse that the "mob" must not yet be
told what this end was, or that the masses were not yet to be won
over to it, does not hold. If the masses could not yet be interested in the actual end of the movement, the movement itself
was premature, and then, even were the means attained, they
would not lead to the desired end. In the hands of a body of
working-men not yet able to understand their historical mission,
universal suffrage might do more harm than good, and productive
co-operative societies with State-credit could only benefit the
existing powers of the State, and provide it with a prætorian
guard. But if the body of working-men was sufficiently developed to understand the end of the movement, then this should
have been openly declared. It need not have even then been represented as an immediate aim, to be realised there and then. Not
only the leaders, however, but every one of the followers that were
led ought to have known what was the end these means were to
attain, and that they were only means to that end. The public
would have been no more incensed than they were by the struggle
to attain the means alone. Lassalle himself points out how subtle
is the instinct of the governing classes, when it is a question of
their own existence. "Individuals," he rightly says, in this connection, "may be deceived, classes *never*."

Those who consider what I have said above as doctrinaire may
be referred to the history of the movement under Lassalle, and
after him. To the consideration of that history I now proceed.

CHAPTER VIII.

LASSALLE AS AGITATOR AND LEADER OF THE ASSOCIATION.

IT is impossible, without expanding this sketch into a large volume, to enter into all the details of the Lassalle agitation. I must confine myself rather to indicating the general features of the movement.

The "Open Reply Letter" for a time only partially produced the effect which Lassalle had promised himself from it. He might well write to his friend Gustav Lewy, at Düsseldorf : "The whole thing reads so easily that it must at once seem to the working-man as if he had known it all for years." The pamphlet was indeed a masterpiece for agitation ; instructive and yet not dry ; eloquent without phrase-mongering, full of warmth, and yet written with the most trenchant logic. But—the workers meanwhile did not even read it ; only where the soil had already been prepared, did it take root among them. This, as we have already seen, was the case at Leipzig ; so, too, at Frankfort-on-the-Maine, in a few of the larger towns and industrial centres of the Rhine, and in Hamburg. To some extent political refugees who had returned had carried on a Socialistic propaganda in a small way, while, to some extent—especially along the Rhine—the traditions of the Socialist propaganda before and during the Revolution of 1848, revived again. But the mass of the workers who took part in the political movement, for a long time yet remained unmoved by this appeal, and looked upon Lassalle in the same way as he was regarded by most of the leaders of the Progressist Party— as a cat's-paw of the reaction.

For so far as the Progressist Party in Prussia and outside Prussia, is concerned, the "Reply Letter" had certainly raised a perfect storm—that is, a storm of indignation, of passionate resentment. They had felt themselves so great, so paramount in their role of knights of the threatened rights of the people—and now, suddenly, from the left, a voice cried out that they had no claim to this title, that they had proved themselves unworthy of the confidence hitherto placed in them by the people, and that, therefore, everyone who really cared for freedom, and especially every working-man, must turn his back upon them. No fighting party will tolerate such an accusation, least of all when it is in such a position as that of the Progressist Party at this time. The feuds between it and the Prussian Government had gradually attained such dimensions that a forcible solution of the conflict seemed well-nigh unavoidable ; at any rate, one must be prepared for the worst. To the contention of the Government organs that the Progressist Party had not the people really at their back, they had hitherto been able to reply with contempt and scorn, that the masses, the thoughtful people who cared for politics, were unanimously with them, and confident of this, they had always used more and more threatening language. For though the Progressists might not have a great desire to make a revolution, they were by no means chary of threatening with one.[1]

And precisely at such a moment as this they were to allow a man, who spoke as a democrat, as an opponent of the Government, to reproach them with having betrayed the cause of the people, to look on quietly while this man sought to gather the workers around himself under a new banner ? To expect this was to expect the superhuman.

Why, the very sense of self-preservation forced the Progressists

---

[1] I can still remember this period very well although I was only a school-boy ; my first political impressions date from it. In school, in the playground—everywhere—in those days we talked politics, and, of course, we boys only repeated in our own way what we heard at home, in our surroundings. My class-mates belonged to the middle-class ; my play-fellows to the proletariat ; but the former were as convinced as the latter that a revolution " must come," for " my father says so, too." Every expression of the Progressist leaders that could be construed into a reference to the revolution, was triumphantly passed from mouth to mouth ; so, too, the satirical verses on the King and his ministers, etc.

to do their utmost to prevent the Lassalle agitation from gaining ground. And subsequent criticism has to do only with the manner of their counter-attack—not with the attack itself. The former was so natural it cannot be considered as a reproach to them—but the manner of their counter-attack can only be described in two words —beneath contempt. That they represented Lassalle as a cat's paw for the reaction, is really the very least they can be reproached with. For after all it cannot be denied that Lassalle's "Reply Letter" just then brought grist to the mill of the Prussian Government. But instead of confining themselves to attacking Lassalle where they had a strong case against him, they fastened, for their attack, upon those points where they were weak, and with this proved themselves so impotent, that their helplessness would almost provoke pity—but for the fact that it was accompanied with such colossal self-assertion. To Lassalle's one-sided concept of the State, they opposed an absolutely ridiculous negation of all the social-political duties of the State. To his theory of the iron law of wages—based as we have seen upon a partial misapprehension—they opposed the feeblest glorification of the bourgeois-capitalist system of competition. In their blind rage they so completely forgot the actual condition of affairs, everything that they themselves had formerly said in regard to the evil effects of capitalist production, that they even justified the exaggerations of Lassalle by the absurdity of their own contentions. From petty-bourgeois opponents of capitalism, Schulze-Delitzsch and Co. suddenly became its panegyrists. We need only compare the passages from Schulze-Delitzsch's work, published in 1858, quoted earlier in this volume (pp. 8, 9), with the statements in his "Kapitel zu einem deutschen Arbeiter Katechismus"[1] — a collection of six lectures, the later ones of which were meant to annihilate Lassalle critically before the Berlin working-men. While in the former work the helping to cut down the profits of the employer was eulogised as one of the most admirable results of the self-help associations, in the latter Schulze - Delitzsch declared that "science knew nothing of such a thing as em-

[1] "Chapter towards a German Workers' Catechism."

ployer's profits," and consequently, of course, knew nothing of any antagonism between the wages of labour and employer's profits. They recognised only "(*a*) wages of enterprise and (*b*) profits of capital." (See Schulze-Delitzsch ; *Kapitel*, etc., p. 153.) One did not even need to be a Lassalle in order to cope with such " science " as that.

Yet, despite his intellectual superiority, despite his powerful rhetoric, Lassalle was not so successful in his campaign against the Progressists as he expected to be. There was not then the remotest idea of the " Open Reply Letter " having an effect like that of the Theses Luther nailed to the church door at Wittenberg —an effect which Lassalle, however, as he says in the letter to his friend Lewy, already quoted, had expected.

On the 19th May, 1863, at a public meeting at Frankfort-on-the-Maine, held at the conclusion of the "Maine District Workers' Congress," Lassalle, who had attended the Congress, which sat two days, and who delivered a speech of four hours, got a resolution passed pledging those present to do their utmost to start a General German Working-men's Association on Lassallean lines. Thereupon, on the 23rd May, 1863, the " General German Working-men's Association " had been formed at Leipzig, when delegates from ten towns (Hamburg, Leipzig, Frankfort - on - the - Maine, Harburg, Cologne, Düsseldorf, Mainz, Elberfeld, Barmen, Solingen), were present, the rules having been drawn up by Lassalle, together with a friend of his, the Democratic Progressist member of Parliament, Ziegler.

In conformity with these rules, the organisation was a strictly centralised one ; which was due partly to the German laws affecting association, and partly to the fact that the founding of a General Workers' Insurance Society had originally been intended. This idea had been dropped, but Lassalle retained the rules that affected himself solely, more especially those which guaranteed the personal prerogatives of, and gave positively dictatorial powers to, the president, who was, into the bargain, to be elected for five years. There were certainly already some signs of opposition to these rules at this first assembly for the foundation of the Association, but in the face of Lassalle's express wish that the rules should be accepted without alteration, the opposition fell through. By an all but unanimous vote (only one delegate, York from Harburg, voted against him) Lassalle was elected president, and after some hesitation, the assembly having further given him power to elect as often, and for any term of office he chose, a vice-president, he accepted the presidentship. By virtue of this he became the acknowledged leader of the new movement; but for a long time to come the movement was limited to a very small number of adherents. Three months after its foundation the General German Working-men's Association numbered scarcely 900. In itself this would have been no mean success, but Lassalle had counted upon figures very different from these. He did not want to be the leader of a propagandist society, but the head of a popular movement. Only the masses kept aloof from the new organisation.

Lassalle was a splendid worker. At times he was capable of developing a positively colossal energy; but it was not given to him to do steady, solid, persistent work. The Association was barely six weeks old when the new president started upon a long holiday of many months, first going to Switzerland, and then to the North Sea. It is true that Lassalle was not inactive during his travels. He kept up a lively correspondence, tried to win over all sorts of notabilities to the Association, and was not very particular in his choice. But the main thing—the agitation among the masses— he left severely alone. Farther, he did not even, strangely enough, seek to secure for the Association at least a good weekly organ, although he had the means to do so. He contented himself with the occasional subventioning of small papers—the *Nordstern*, published in Hamburg, by the old free-lance Bruhn, and the Leipzig *Zeitgeist*,—by the way a very doubtful organ—edited by the litterateur, Ed. Löwenthal; subventions which kept these papers for a time above water, but did not prevent them from constantly hovering between life and death.

Like the mass of the workers, most of the advanced Democrats, and middle-class Socialists, whom Lassalle invited to join the

Association, kept away from it. A large number of these people were, as I have already pointed out, steeped in philistinism or, at any rate, were on the high road to it ; others were prevented by a vague, personal distrust of Lassalle from openly declaring for him, whilst others again thought the time very inopportune for an attack of the left wing upon the Progressists. And even those who did join the Association, for the most part contented themselves with simple membership, and for the rest remained passive.

As a set-off against these, however, other members of the Association, especially those belonging to the working-class, agitated the more energetically, while the secretary of the Association, Julius Vahlteich, showed a positively feverish activity in trying to get new members for the organisation. But their success was by no means commensurate with their efforts. On the one hand the indifference of the still undeveloped masses of the workers, on the other, the all-absorbing interest of the hour—the national movement, together with the constitutional struggle in Prussia—seemed almost insurmountable difficulties. In many places, indeed, the members of the Association eagerly discussed the question whether some sort of bait of a non-political nature, as, *e.g.*, the starting of benefit funds, etc., should not be offered in order to attract members.

Lassalle himself was at one time inclined to enter into the discussion of this question—see his letter of the 29th August, 1863, to the secretary of the Association, quoted by B. Becker in his " History of the Working Class Agitation," p. 83—but he gave it up again, because he saw that were this done, the character of the Association must necessarily be changed. It would have ceased to provide a political machine always ready to hand, and this was the only value it had in Lassalle's eyes.

While still at the Baths, Lassalle had worked out the main ideas of a speech with which he intended recommencing the agitation on his return,—to begin with at the Rhine where the position had proved most favourable to him. This was the speech : " Die Feste, die Presse, und der Frankfurter Abgeordnetentag." [1]

---

[1] " The Fêtes, the Press, and the Frankfort Congress of Members of Parliament."

This speech, which Lassalle delivered from the 20th to the 29th September, at Barmen, Solingen, and Düsseldorf, marks the turning-point in his agitation. What influences had been brought to bear upon him during the summer months, it would hardly be possible to prove, but we shall not be far wrong in concluding that they were those of the Countess Hatzfeld and her connections. The Countess had, naturally enough, an even greater desire to see Lassalle successful than he himself had; for her all interest in Socialism was completely absorbed in interest in Lassalle, through whom, indeed, she had first become socialistically inclined. Assuredly, also, she was only moved by her great affection for Lassalle, when she urged him on to steps which could only serve to satisfy his personal ambition, and which could not but very seriously compromise the movement itself. But to the Countess the movement was Lassalle, and Lassalle the movement; and she looked at all things from the point of view of what she believed to be Lassalle's interests. Such disinterested friends are, however, as a rule, of very doubtful value. And when they are into the bargain, by education, social position, etc., warped with special class prejudice, and when they have no independent sphere of action, their co-operation often works more dangerously than poison. They foster all the failings and weaknesses of the object of their love; they constantly work upon his sensibility by calling attention to every injustice apparently done to him; and more bitterly than the injured person himself, do they thirst to be avenged for the injustice done; they hound, they egg on, they intrigue—always with the best intentions—but to the greatest detriment of him whom they mean to serve.

The Countess Hatzfeld was, in her way, an able woman, who, very inferior as she was to Lassalle in knowledge and energy, was yet his superior in experience. Where his passions did not stand in the way, he attached great importance to her advice,—and her advice was doubly effective when it chimed in with his passions. In a letter written to the Countess towards the end of his life, he says to her that, after all, it was really she who had induced him to accept the presidency of the General German Working-men's

Association. This must certainly not be taken literally. Even without the Countess, Lassalle would probably have accepted the presidentship. But in such situations one likes especially to let one's good friends talk one over into doing what one has a mind to, because it seems to lessen one's responsibility. So the Countess probably soothed Lassalle's scruples, and it is more than likely that she did this by preferring to call his attention to matters then impending in the higher circles of Prussia. I need but remind my readers of Lassalle's statement in his defence at the trial for high treason, that from the first day in which he began his agitation, he had *known* that Prince Bismarck would grant universal suffrage, and his further statement that when he issued the "Open Reply Letter," it was "clear" to him that "great foreign conflicts were imminent, conflicts which would make it impossible to ignore the masses." It is true that he here tries to represent this as a matter which everyone who was carefully watching events must have known. But from his letters to Marx, we have seen how much he allowed his political acts to be influenced by the "information" given him from "diplomatic sources" as to what was going on in governmental circles.

The Countess had certainly been even more disappointed than Lassalle himself at the slow progress of the General German Working-men's Association. Led by all the educational influences of her life to trust to the use of intrigue and scheming, she was now also bound to think of attaining by roundabout means what it was difficult to obtain in an open struggle. In this design she found only too ready support in Lassalle's tendency to win success on which he had once set his mind, at any price, in his reckless temperament and his enormous self-esteem.

In how far the threads by which Lassalle was led to the palace of Prince von Bismarck were already knotted together it is impossible at this time of day to say. But both the words which, as he was preparing his speech, "*The Fêtes, the Press,*" etc., for print, he addressed to his friend, Lewy, "*What I am writing here I am writing for only a few people in Berlin,*" and above all the subject-matter of the speech itself prove that at least these threads were being eagerly spun. The speech is interlarded with attacks upon the Progressist Party, which in certain cases are very much exaggerated, while, on the contrary, Herr von Bismarck is positively flattered. If hitherto the democrat and the socialist in Lassalle had always mastered the demagogue vein in him, here the demagogue masters them both.

In June, 1863, after dismissing the Landtag, the Prussian Government had issued the notorious Press Regulations, which empowered the Government officials, after giving two warnings, to prohibit, " provisionally or permanently," the further publication of any Prussian newspaper or periodical " for pursuing a line of conduct dangerous to the public weal." The Liberal press, exclusively in the hands of private individuals, had thereupon, for the most part, preferred to say nothing more whatever about internal politics as long as the Press Regulations were in force. This was certainly anything but bold, but it was not such vile treachery to their own cause as Lassalle represented. Lassalle intentionally overlooked the fact that in issuing the Press Regulations it had been Bismarck's deliberate intention to ruin the opposition papers that were objectionable to him *commercially*, in order to replace them with a press of his own, or one more agreeable to himself. In the preamble to the Press Regulations it was distinctly stated :—

" The direct counter-effect against the influences of the above— (*i.e.*, the Liberal press)—*by means of the Conservative press*, can only partially attain the desired results, because most of the opposition organs, through long years of habit on the part of the public, *and through the commercial side of the said organs, have a circulation which it is not easy to combat.*"

If, therefore, the Liberal papers did not run the risk of being prohibited, the Government also had no possibility of smuggling other journals into their place, or of stealing their advertisements. The one object of the measure was therefore defeated by this temporary silence on internal politics. And not less did it defeat the second directly political object. In his speech, Lassalle says that if the Liberal press allowed itself to be suppressed, if the Philistine had been unable to get his customary paper at breakfast, the exasperation among the people against the Press Regulations would have grown to such a pitch that the Government would have been obliged to give in. Meanwhile, the exasperation was not the less if the Philistine continued to get his customary morning paper, while its contents daily demonstrated to him that his organ was gagged ; when he got his paper, but without the beloved leading article.

Moreover, the Press Regulations were a measure that could not be kept up after the Landtag had assembled. It was a provisional measure, and while it lasted there was no reason whatever why the Liberals should—as Lassalle expresses it—for the love of Bismarck, " die with honour."

The anger of the Government was, of course, not little, and its organs naturally reflected this anger. Lassalle thus expresses this : " Even (!) the reactionary papers could, at this time, hardly find words to sufficiently express their astonishment and indignation at this attitude." And as a proof he quotes the *Berliner Revue*, the organ of the most reactionary mugwumps. Of course, the reactionaries resorted to the device of hiding their attacks upon the Liberal press beneath a thin socialistic mantle, and pretended to attack it because of its capitalist character. And yet, instead of protesting against this misrepresentation of the Socialist idea, and of repudiating all connection with it, Lassalle actually played up to the Bismarckists by representing their false coin to the workers as pure gold.

Certainly, the fact that the press of to-day is a business concern is a great evil, a mighty factor in the corruption of public life. But, so long as capitalist private property exists, it will scarcely be possible to obviate this—least of all, by restrictive laws. So far as this can be remedied to-day, it can only be by freedom of the press. But of this the Prussian Government would not hear, and Lassalle supported them. For while advocating complete freedom of the press, he at the same time declared that such freedom would be powerless to alter the nature of the press, if, at the same time, the right to publish advertisements were not prohibited. For then the press would cease to be a lucrative business speculation, and only such men would write for the newspapers as were fighting for the well-being and intellectual interests of the people.

Is any particular argument needed to show how absolutely ineffective this remedy would be? Lassalle had only to look beyond the frontiers of the Prussian State, to England and to France, to convince himself of his error. In England, the advertising system formed, and still forms, a very essential source of income to the press; while in France, though the insertion of advertisements in newspapers was not directly prohibited, it was made almost impossible, and was reduced to a minimum, by a very high tax. Was the French press any better on that account than the English? Less at the service of Capitalism, less corrupt than the latter? Not a whit. The absence of advertisements, on the contrary, made it very much easier for Bonaparte to corrupt the press to his own ends, and, on the other hand, it has not prevented the political press of France from rendering far greater service to the big financiers than the political press of England has done.

For all that, Lassalle was, in this portion of his speech at least, touching on a question which must certainly be designated as one of the sores of our modern public life. Even though the time was badly chosen, though the remedy was of problematical value, in itself the fact remains, that the press, with or without advertisements, is becoming more and more a capitalist institution, a cancerous growth to which the attention of the working-class must be called, if they are to free themselves from the influences of the capitalist organs.

But altogether beside the mark was what Lassalle said of the fêtes which the Progressists held in 1863 in defiance of Bismarck. He must have known that the fêtes were nothing but propagandist meetings, but demonstrations against the Government, such as had been held, under like conditions, in France and England. Had he wished to criticise them, he should have shown that by fêtes alone nothing can be done ; that if they stopped at these the cause of the people against the Government was not advanced a single step. But instead of doing this he contented himself with repeating the phrases of the Government press on the fêtes, and even exaggerating the scorn beneath which the latter tried to conceal their vexation. No one who is intimately acquainted with the history of the Prussian constitutional struggles of the year 1863 can read this passage of Lassalle's speech without disapproval.

The third part of the speech, the criticism of the Congress of the German members of Parliament that had met at Frankfort-on-Maine in the summer of 1863, would have been justified if Lassalle, at the very moment when he was reproaching the Progressists for coquetting with the German Princes, in order to frighten Herr von Bismarck—we have seen how in his "Open reply letter" he had twitted them with the "Dogma of Prussian Supremacy" and had represented Prussia as the most reactionary of the German States—it would have been justified if, at the same time, Lassalle had not been playing the same game as the Progressists, only that he was coquetting with the other side. His entire speech does not contain a single word against Bismarck and the Prussian Government, but is full of direct and indirect flattery addressed to them. He represents them as ignoring the resolutions of the Chamber " with the quiet smile of genuine contempt," and provides Bismarck with the certificate that he is " a man," while the Progressists were old women. One more passage in the speech bears witness to Lassalle's change of front.

The leader of the *National Verein*, Herr von Bennigsen, had closed the Congress with the following words, and it may be as well to recall them once again. " The violence of the *Volkspartei*, and the hide-bound nature of rulers, had often led to revolutionary upheavals. But the German people were not only unanimous, but also so moderate in their demands, that the German National Party—which *desired no revolution,* and *which could make none*—could not be held responsible if after it another party should appear, which, because no reform was any longer possible, should resort to a revolution."

To any one who can read, this declaration, though a very weak-kneed threat, is yet a threat of a revolution. " We don't want a revolution—God forbid—we wash our hands of it, *but*, if you don't give in, the revolution will come all the same, and then you'll only have yourselves to thank for it." A very cowardly way of threatening when you have the whole nation at your back, but, unfortunately, also a very common way of threatening—so common that, as I have said, it is impossible to misunderstand the meaning of the declaration. But what does Lassalle do? He pretends not to have understood the threat, and he makes this pretence not in order to challenge the Progressists to speak out more decidedly, but in order to threaten them in the event of a revolution or a *coup d'état*. He quotes the above passage from Herr von Bennigsen, and adds the following pronunciamento : " Let us lift up our arms and pledge ourselves, if this revolution should come about, whether in this way or in that, to remember that the Progressists and members of the *National Verein* to the last declared they wanted no revolution ! Pledge yourselves to do this, raise your hands on high."

And " the whole meeting raised its hands in great excitement," we are told in the report of the speech—which Lassalle himself edited.

What did this threat, this " remembering," mean? It was almost impossible to explain otherwise than that the Progressists were to be, if not directly attacked, yet left in the lurch in the event of a violent conflict arising " in this way or in that." But such a threat, and at such a moment, could have but one result —instead of forcing the Progressists forward, to make them yet more pusillanimous.

At a meeting at Solingen there was a bloody conflict. A number of Progressists, who had attempted to interrupt Lassalle, were attacked with knives by some of his fanatical adherents. In consequence of this, the Burgomaster, half an hour later, dissolved the meeting. Thereupon Lassalle, followed by a cheering crowd, hurried to the telegraph office, and sent off to Bismarck the well-known telegram, beginning with the words : " Progressist Burgomaster has just, at the head of ten gendarmes armed with bayonets, and several policemen with drawn swords, dissolved a working-men's meeting called by me, without any legal justification ; " and ending, " I ask for the severest, promptest, legal satisfaction."

Even taking into consideration everything that is to be said in Lassalle's excuse—his bitterness about the repeated attacks upon him by the Progressists, his disappointment at the comparatively small success of his agitation, his profound distaste for the cowardly tactics of the Progressists, his one-sided but still sincere antagonism to the liberal economic doctrines—in short, however much we may try to put ourselves in his place at this time, still one thing unquestionably results from this telegram, taken in connection with the speech described above—that when Lassalle returned to Germany he had already lost his mental anchorage, had lost, if I may so say, his *standpoint.* No conservative would have been forgiven such a telegram ; far less a man who had been proud to call himself a revolutionist, and who certainly, in his heart, still believed himself to be one. If no other considerations did, the simplest feeling of tact should have prevented Lassalle from making an appeal for State-force, that began with a political denunciation.

And even were it possible to excuse this telegram on the ground of his excitement at the breaking up of the meeting, other steps soon followed, undertaken with the coolest deliberation, which were as diametrically opposed to the political principle which Lassalle claimed to represent. Here, but one example, one which is, moreover, closely connected with the events to which I have referred.

Some working-men, who were said to have used their knives at the Solingen meeting, were, in the spring of 1864, condemned to several months' imprisonment. And it was Lassalle, who in all seriousness, and repeatedly, suggested that the condemned men, supported by a general address of the working-classes, should present a petition for mercy to the *King of Prussia*. Think of the Lassalle, who only a few years before (see page 57 of this volume) had written that it was only in Berlin that to his grief he had seen

" how little the people in Prussia were dis monarchied ; " who at Frankfort-on-Maine had exclaimed : " I have no desire and no call to speak to any others than to Democrats " ; he, whose duty as leader of the new movement it especially was to set his followers the example of democratic dignity, urged them to beg for mercy from the King of Prussia. However, the workers proved themselves more tactful in this case than their leader. On the 20th April, 1864, the Solingen delegate of the workmen, Klings, announced that there was a general objection to Lassalle's proposal. All the chief members of the Association had declared against it. " The two from here who have been condemned belong to the most outspoken Working-men's Party, and even if the sentence were four years, it would be impossible to induce them to present a petition for mercy, because it goes against their convictions to be indebted to His Majesty."

This opposition awoke Lassalle's democratic conscience, and he wrote to Klings that the refusal of the people filled him with great pride. He did not yet, however, give up his idea of an address to the King, but tried to prove that even without the petition for mercy from the condemned men, this might be very advantageous. " *Perhaps,* too," he actually writes, " the following advantage might ensue, that if the address were signed by many thousands of workers, this step might be so interpreted in the highest circles—without at all binding us—that they would feel the more encouraged, on the next opportunity, to proceed with the introduction of universal and direct suffrage : a step which, as the accompanying leader from the *ministerial* organ (*Nord-deutsche Allgemeine Zeitung*) shows, they are just now again considering." However, even this prospect was unable to convince the Solingen workers of the fitness of the step recommended, and so the movement was spared this humiliation.

When, in the beginning of October, 1863, Lassalle returned to Berlin, he set about winning over the capital to his cause with the utmost zeal. He drew up an appeal " To the Workers of Berlin," of which he published 16,000 copies, a portion of which he had distributed gratis among the working-men of Berlin.

Although the appeal was very effectively written, and the connecting of it with the garbled reports of the Rhenish meetings in the Berlin Progressist press (*Volks Zeitung* and *Reform*) was especially able, yet its success was at first a very modest one. Lassalle was unable to hold any large meeting without its being broken up by the Progressists; and when, at one of his meetings, by order of the Berlin authorities, Lassalle was arrested, some fanatical working-men actually applauded. And even those who, under the effect of Lassalle's lectures and writings, had their names entered in the books of the Association, soon dropped out again, so that the Association, which, in the beginning of December, 1863, had in Berlin had over 200 members, in February, 1864, counted barely three dozen, the greater number of whom, moreover, were not working-men.

Besides the agitation, Lassalle was much occupied with his lawsuits and other conflicts with the authorities. For, however agreeable his agitation, so far as it was directed against the Progressist Party might be to the Bismarck ministry, this yet knew well enough that it had not in Lassalle a supporter who would allow himself to be used as a complaisant tool. It could only be agreeable to the ministry, therefore, if the lower officials continued to overwhelm Lassalle with prosecutions, etc. By this means the ministry was in a position either, at the right time, to get rid of an obnoxious firebrand, or, perhaps, even to "bring him to his knees," after all. However this may be, the Düsseldorf Public Prosecutor had the speech "*The Fêtes, the Press,*" etc., confiscated, and brought a charge against Lassalle of violating Secs. 100 and 101 of the Prussian Code [Inciting to disorder and propagating false statements, with the intention of discrediting regulations of the authorities]. The prosecution caused Lassalle infinite worry, and after a sentence of one year's imprisonment pronounced in contumaciam by the first court, ended, after his appeal to a higher court, in a sentence of six months' imprisonment. For the pamphlet "To the Berlin Workers," the Berlin authorities brought a charge of high treason against Lassalle, and, as I have already mentioned, had him arrested, when, however, he was liberated on bail. It is possible that both the charge and the preliminary arrest may have been due to the personal spite of the Attorney, Von Schelling, whom Lassalle had so belaboured a year before at his trial before the *Stadtgericht*. At the trial that took place on the 12th March, 1864, before the *Stadtgericht* of Berlin, the Public Prosecutor asked no less than that Lassalle should be sentenced to three years' penal servitude and five years' police surveillance. The Court, however, so far as the charge of high treason was concerned, dismissed the case, and referred the minor charges of breaches of the Code, brought by the authorities, to the Courts competent to deal with them.

Lassalle's speech in his defence at this trial is an important document for the history of his agitation. Before considering it, however, a big socio-political work of Lassalle's must be mentioned. It was published at the end of January, 1864, and must rank as his foremost work in the way of agitation. This is his polemic "Herr Bastiat-Schulze von Delitzsch, der Ökonomische Julian, oder Kapital und Arbeit." [1]

I have already referred, in passing, to the lectures delivered in the spring of 1863 by Herr Schulze-Delitzsch to the Berlin Working-men's Association, and published under the title " Kapitel zu einem deutschen Arbeiter Katechismus," as a counterblast to the Lassallean agitation. These lectures, a re-hash of the tritest commonplaces of liberal political economy, provided Lassalle with a welcome opportunity for annihilating—theoretically—Herr Schulze-Delitzsch, and with him the party which revered him as their economic hero. If we bear in mind that Lassalle had never been able to do any systematic economic work, and that at the very time when he wished to set about the preliminary studies for his book on economics he was prevented from doing so by his practical agitation ; if, further, we bear in mind that while Lassalle was writing the "Bastiat-Schulze," he was constantly interrupted by his lawsuits, and the labour of managing the Association, one cannot but see in this book a fresh proof of the extraordinary talent, the marvellous

---

[1] " Herr Bastiat-Schulze von Delitzsch, the Julian of Economy, or Capital and Labour."

versatility and elasticity of Lassalle's mind. It is true that the
" Bastiat-Schulze " at the same time bears traces of the conditions
under which it was written. However much the popularity of
the pamphlet is helped by its polemical form, the circumstances
under which this controversy arose—the extreme irritation of
Lassalle, that was all the greater because he felt keenly that he
was placing himself in a more and more false position, his disillusions on the one hand, and his efforts on the other, to blind
himself as to these disillusions—were fatal to the *tone* of the
polemic. But intrinsically, too, the work is by no means always up
to the level of its subject ; it frequently degenerates into small
verbal quibbling, which, moreover, is not always accurate.[1] Then,
too, the fundamental and theoretical part of the work, brilliant as
it is in many points, is not free from contradictions. Taken all
in all, however, the " Bastiat-Schulze " has still the great merit
of having largely advanced the historical sense, and the understanding of the deeper problems of political economy amongst the
German workers. In parts the presentation rises to the height of
the best writings of Lassalle, and in these passages his genius appears once again in its most brilliant light.

[1] Thus, *e.g.*, Lassalle's first objection against " Schulze-Delitzsch,"
that " wants " and the " impulse to satisfy wants," were only " two different expressions for the same thing," is incorrect. Both, as a rule,
coincide, but are by no means the same thing. A few pages later on
Lassalle makes fun of Schulze-Delitzsch because the latter sees the
difference between human and animal labour in this—that the former
labour provides for future wants. He himself, however, falls into the still
greater error of seeing the difference only in this, that man works consciously, and the animal without any such consciousness. And so in many
other passages.

CHAPTER IX.

VAIN ATTEMPTS TO COMPEL IMMEDIATE POLITICAL SUCCESS.—AP-
PROACHING THE REACTIONARY GOVERNMENT OF PRINCE BIS-
MARCK.—LASSALLE'S DEATH.

ALL that Lassalle wrote and said after the "Bastiat-Schulze," gives ever clearer proof of inner lassitude, of mental enerva-tion. His energy is no longer the original energy, the natural result of belief in his own force, and the strength of the cause championed—it is forced. Compare the " *Worker's Pro-gramme*" with the Ronsdorf Speech; the defence speech, " *Science and the Workers*," with his defence in the trial for high treason, and what I have just said will be understood. The inner energy has gone, and violent language replaces it ; logical flourishes replace incontrovertible logical arguments ; instead of convincing, Lassalle takes more and more to declamation. That with which he had but recently reproached the Progressists he now does himself—he intoxicates himself with imaginary successes.

At the trial for high treason, Lassalle, in defending himself against the charge that what underlay his agitation, was the ulti-mate use of physical force, very ably used the picture of Schiller's Wallenstein on the night before his going over to the Swedes, and quoted the verses of the monologue in the first act of " Wallen-stein's Tod " :

> " Wär's möglich ?—Könnt ich nicht mehr wie ich wollte ?
> Nicht mehr zurük, wie mir's beliebt ? " [1]

It is wonderful how these lines fit in with Lassalle's own situa-tion at this time ; how like his position was to that of Wallenstein

---

[1] " Is't possible ?   Could I no more do as I would ?
No more turn back, as I desire ? "

when he speaks these words. He, too, like the Friedländer, had—to use his own image—"done things that he could turn to account *à deux mains.*" He had not contented himself with studying the course of internal and foreign politics objectively, with a view to seizing the right moment for forwarding his own plan of campaign ; he had already begun to treat with the representative of one of the powers against whom he was fighting ; he had entered into direct negotiation with Herr von Bismarck. Assuredly, he too could still say with Wallenstein :

> "Noch ist sie rein, noch ! Das Verbrechen kam
> Nicht über diese Schwelle noch !"[1]

As yet he had broken no pledge. But was he still really free in his inner heart ? Might not the logic of events force him also to consummate the "deed" because he "did not put away temptation from him ? "

That in the winter of 1863 to 1864 Lassalle had repeated and important conferences, *tête-à-tête* with the then Herr von Bismarck, there can now be no doubt whatever. The life long confidante of Lassalle, the Countess Sophie von Hatzfeld, when, in the summer of 1878, Bismarck introduced his gagging Bill against German Social Democracy, on her own initiative told representatives of that party of these facts, adding circumstantial details. When the member of the Reichstag, Bebel, in the sitting of September 16th, 1878, brought the matter before the Reichstag, Bismarck the next day admitted having had interviews with Lassalle, and only made an attempt to deny that they had had reference to any political negotiations. Bebel, on the strength of the communications made by the Countess Hatzfeld, said : " These conversations and negotiations turned upon two different matters : firstly, upon the granting of universal suffrage ; and secondly, upon the granting of State-help to the productive co-operative associations. Prince Bismarck had been completely won over to this plan by Lassalle.

---

[1] " Yet it is pure,—as yet ! For never crime
Has passed across this threshold yet.'

He only refused to introduce universal suffrage until such time as the Schleswig-Holstein war had been satisfactorily concluded, and only refused to push it through *immediately* as Lassalle wished. In consequence of this difference of opinion, serious disagreements arose between Lassalle and Prince Bismarck ; and it was not the latter who broke off the negotiations, but it was, as I must emphatically state, Lassalle who caused the breach, and who declared he could not enter into further negotiations."

To this Bismarck replied : " Our conversations undoubtedly turned upon the question of universal suffrage, but under no circumstances upon an introduction of it. I never in all my life entertained so monstrous an idea as to grant universal suffrage in this way by forcing it upon the Chamber." He had accepted it " with some reluctance " as a " Frankfurt tradition." As to the productive co-operative associations, he was "not even to-day convinced of their inexpedience." Only, the political events at that time had not allowed of the carrying out of the experiments initiated in this direction. Moreover, it was not he but Lassalle who had desired these meetings, who had written to request them, and he, Bismarck, had consented to meet Lassalle's wishes as a mere caprice. " What could Lassalle have offered or given me ? He had nothing at his back. The *do ut des* is at the bottom of all political negotiations, even when one doesn't, for decency's sake, say so. But when one is forced to say to oneself, ' what can you, poor devil, give ?' There was nothing he could have given me as minister."

It is perfectly clear that the man who has " never lied officially " here deals very unofficially with the truth. Lassalle would not have gone to the minister, nor would the latter have repeatedly sent for the " revolutionary Jew "—Bismarck himself admits this may have occurred some four times, while the Countess Hatzfeld maintains that it was oftener, three or four times a week—and have discussed with him for hours together just for the sake of a chat. Further, one has but to read over the speeches of the representatives of the Government in the Chamber, and the articles in the official press of this period, to be convinced how greatly the Bismarck ministry was then taken up with the idea of introducing universal suffrage; and under the then existing circumstances, this could hardly have been done in any other way than by that of royal force. Lassalle himself, in his defence before the *Stadtgerichthof*, quotes some remarks to the same effect, and subsequently adds in connection therewith the celebrated declaration, which can only now that his interviews with Bismarck are known, be rightly appreciated.

"The prosecutor accuses me of wishing to introduce universal and direct suffrage, and thus to *overthrow* the Constitution !

"Well, gentlemen, although I am but a private individual, I may say to you : not only do I *wish* to overthrow the Constitution, but perchance, ere one year shall have passed, I will *have* overthrown it !

"But how ? Without one drop of blood having been shed, without a hand having been raised in violence ! Perchance not another year shall have passed, but universal and direct suffrage will have been introduced by the Government in the most peaceful manner in the world.

"The *strong* hands, gentlemen, can be played with exposed cards ! It is the *strongest* diplomacy that does not need to conceal its calculations with *any* secrecy, because it is founded upon iron necessity.

"And so I proclaim to you, here in this solemn spot, *perchance not another year shall pass —and Herr von Bismarck will have played the rôle of Robert Peel, and universal and direct suffrage shall have been proclaimed !* "

Lassalle certainly adds that he had known this from the beginning, " from the very first day on which, by issuing my 'Reply Letter,' I began this agitation, and it could have escaped no one who looked at the situation with his eyes open." But if it is indubitably true that already in the winter of 1862-1863 the question was being mooted in Government circles, whether it would be possible to break up the Progressist majority in the Chamber, by a change in the electoral law, and to this end they began dabbling in the social question ; [1] yet Lassalle would scarcely have spoken

[1] Let me again remind readers of the attitude taken up by Eichler. The

with such certainty of a speedy introduction of universal suffrage, have constantly recurred to it, unless he had been convinced from his conversations with B'smarck, that, whether introduced before or at the end of the Danish campaign, this measure had been decided upon.

On the other hand, Bismarck's contention that it had never come to any rupture between himself and Lassalle is more credible. The negotiations may have dropped for a time, when Lassalle became convinced that Bismarck wanted to wait events before undertaking this, after all, risky step—and explains why Lassalle always speaks of the possible introduction of the measure within a year's time. But that the relations were not finally broken off, is proved by the fact that Lassalle continued to send, through the secretary of the "General German Working-men's Association," a copy of all his publications, etc., under cover and marked "*private*," to Bismarck.

So, too, we may believe Bismarck that his negotiations with Lassalle could come to no definite settlement, because of the *do ut des.* Of course, matters were not quite as Bismarck would represent them with his churlish, "what can you, poor devil, give? He had nothing he could have offered me as minister." At this time Bismarck was by no means so secure in his position as not to need *every* help he could get, and Lassalle could, all the same, have given him something. The fact was only this, that it was not *enough* to decide Bismarck to yield to Lassalle's importunities. Perhaps, too, this is one of the reasons why Lassalle, after his return to Berlin, exaggerated his successes in a positively

following passage from the conclusion of a speech delivered by Herr Hermann Wagener—the confidant of Bismarck, the inspirer and director of the *Kreuz-Zeitung*—at a meeting of the Prussian Conservative *Volksverein*, on the 2nd November, 1862, is also of interest. "Gentlemen, let us not deceive ourselves, let us learn from our opponents, for they rightly say, if you do not succeed in solving the social question, all your toil and labour will be in vain. I, therefore, conclude with this appeal—let us set about that which we recognise as the task and requirement of the immediate future, let us set about this with even greater energy, let us set about it not only at election times,"

morbid manner ; he, who had written so late as July, 1863, to
Vahlteich : " You cannot allow our delegates to tell untruths.
So you cannot, therefore, ask them to speak of 10,000 men, when
perhaps we haven't got 1000. We may be silent upon this point,
but is not meet that we should lie." He now wished, at all costs,
to *seem* to possess power, even though he had no actual masses
to lead. But Bismarck was probably kept sufficiently well posted
by other informants as to the real condition of the movement.

And there was also another side to this " giving." Bismarck
can hardly have doubted even for a single moment that in Lassalle
he would have a political ally only for so long, and in so far as
the alliance would be to the advantage of Lassalle and his political
ends : in other words, that Lassalle would do by him exactly as
he would do by Lassalle—*i.e.*, turn mercilessly against him as
soon as he had got what he wanted out of him. His first inter-
view with Lassalle must have convinced him that the latter was
not—what Rodbertus once well called Bucher, " a fish without
bones "—but that, on the contrary, he had very portentous bones
and maw. The bait of some small office—not to speak of money
—was useless in the case. Universal suffrage once assured,
Lassalle might easily become very unpleasant—so why be over-
hasty ? Anyhow, Lassalle's agitation was being turned more and
more fiercely and one-sidedly against the Liberal Party, and this
was, for the time being, all Bismarck wanted.

In his defence speech—" *Die Wissenschaft und die Arbeiter*," [1]
delivered on the 16th January, 1863, Lassalle had declared :

" Can any one even assert that with us the three-class electoral
system is to be laid at the door of the possessing classes, of the
German bourgeoisie ? . . . It is the Prussian Government alone,
not the possessing classes in Prussia, which for all time, and before
all the world, must bear the blame and responsibility for enforc-
ing the three-class electoral system." And : " Bourgeoisie and
workers, we are members of one people, and quite united against
our oppressors," *i.e.*, against the Government.

But before the *Stadtgerichthof*, on the 12th March, 1864,

---

[1] " Science and the Workers."

the constitutional conflict in Prussia has become to him only a
struggle between the monarchy and a "clique." To this "clique"
the monarchy could not yield, but "it might well call the
people upon the scene, and trust to them. To do this, it need
but call to mind its origin, for all monarchy has originally been
the monarchy of the people."

" A Louis-Philippe monarchy, a monarchy created by the
bourgeoisie, certainly could not do this ; but a monarchy that
still stands as kneaded out of its original dough, leaning upon THE
HILT OF THE SWORD, might quite certainly do this, if it determined
to pursue truly great, national, and democratic aims."

This is the language of Cæsarism, and during the course of his
speech, Lassalle even intensified it by representing the existing
Constitution as a boon conferred upon the bourgeoisie by the
monarchy. But no one "cares to let his own boon be twisted
into a rope wherewith to strangle himself, and no one can be blamed
for this, and, therefore, neither should the monarchy be blamed."
Constantly driven back upon ostensible "right," the monarchy
had "remembered that it was more fitting to its position to rely
upon *true* right, and to marshal the people upon the stage, than
to yield to a clique, and to allow a handful of individuals to
twist its own boon into a rope, wherewith to strangle it." So
would he, Lassalle, speak on the day when the monarchy should
have overthrown the Constitution, and have introduced universal
suffrage, if he were accused of being the intellectual originator of
this overthrow of the Constitution.

Lassalle had now got so far that he not only did the reaction a
passing service by the existence of his agitation, which, under certain
conditions, was unavoidable. He fell more and more into the habit
of speaking the language of the reactionists. Truly he could still
cry with Wallenstein :

> " Beim grossen Gott des Himmels ! Es war nicht
> Mein Ernst, beschlossene Sache war es nie ! "[1]

> [1] " By the Great God of Heaven ! It was not
> In earnest. It was never so resolved,"

He was playing with the reaction, believed he was using it for his own ends, and that at a given moment he could shake it off with one wrench. In this sense it was that he once spoke to the Countess Hatzfeld of Bismarck as *his* "delegate." But he forgot that there is a logic of facts which is stronger than even the strongest individual will, and that inasmuch as he was *playing* for success, instead of trusting to the very strength of the movement itself, and of devoting his energies exclusively to it, he had, according to his own theory, already, to some extent, partially given up that movement.

In fact, to return once more to the already quoted essay of Lassalle on the fundamental idea of his "Franz von Sickingen": with the *volte-face* performed since his return from the waters, Lassalle had arrived at exactly the same tactics which in this essay he had designated as the "moral guilt" of Franz von Sickingen. It is worthy of note how accurately Lassalle there foreshadowed his own fate. He too had come to that "self-complacent good sense," which seeks to attain revolutionary aims by *diplomatic* means; he had assumed a mask in order to deceive his antagonist—the Prussian Government—but, in fact, he deceived not it, but the mass of the people, without whom he was nothing; the movement itself remained limited to a small group of personal friends. And as Lassalle writes of Sickingen that, "this great diplomatist and realist, who had carefully calculated everything beforehand, and wished to entirely exclude chance, is at last *forced* by the most accidental of chances to lose everything," and "while the calculation based upon this delusion was doomed to failure through the semblance of chance and of the non-essential in the existing condition of things, the ultimate decision, instead of proceeding as he wished from what had been prepared, proceeded from the first unlooked-for chance."[1] So, too, Lassalle finds himself forced now to reckon only with chance, and to make everything in home and foreign politics dependent upon chance constellations. Lassalle played, trusting to his real

[1] See No. 45, 1890-91, of the *Neue Zeit*, p. 588, etc., where I have published this essay.

ability.   But he forgot that the game is to him who has the best
chance of wearing out his opponent, to him who holds the most
trumps in the political game,—therefore, to him who can command the greatest number of really powerful factors.   And as in
this case, Bismarck was in this position and not Lassalle, it was
inevitable that in the long run Lassalle should become Bismarck's
"delegate," rather than Bismarck his.

Such was the situation when Lassalle delivered the Ronsdorf
Address :   "*Die Agitation des Allgemeinen Deutschen Arbeiter-
Vereins und das Versprechen des Königs von Preussen.*"[1]   It was
his last, and, at the same time, the weakest of his agitation speeches,
conceived solely with a view to external effect.   How very conscious Lassalle was of the weakness of this speech is proved by
the published version of it, edited by himself : this is full of
interpolated remarks as to the effect of certain passages—crutches
which a sound lecture can well dispense with, and that would
indeed mar the impression of a really pregnant speech.   The
Ronsdorf Address has none of the qualities of Lassalle's early
agitation speeches, while on the contrary, it emphasises all their
defects.

Moreover, the speech is not merely inherently weak, its tendency also is more reprehensible than anything Lassalle had
until then said or written.

Some Silesian weavers, impelled by their misery, and encouraged
by the social demagogy of the Feudal Party, had sent a deputation to Berlin, to petition the King of Prussia for help against the
wrongs under which they suffered.   And at last, as the employees
of a Progressist manufacturer were concerned, they had, on
Bismarck's instance, been received by the King.   In answer to
their complaints, they had been told that the King had instructed
his ministers " to prepare to render them some legal redress, so
far as this was possible, with all despatch and energy."

That Lassalle should represent this step of the Silesian weavers,
and the reception of their deputation by the King, as a result of

[1] " The Agitation of the General German Working-men's Association,
and the Promise of the King of Prussia."

his agitation, no one—exaggerated as the claim is—will find any great fault with. This, like so many other exaggerations in his Address, is to be explained by Lassalle's position. But Lassalle did not content himself with this. He placed such a construction upon the reception of the deputation by the King, and upon the King's words, as could only result for the time being in a glorification of the King and his Government. He reads the workingmen a report from the semi-official *Zeidler'schen Korrespondenz* on the reception of the deputation by the King, and reads those very passages that are most favourable to the monarchy—as he expressly says in the printed version of the speech—"in the most impressive tone, and accompanied with the most effective gestures of the hand."[1]

In the King's words, he declared, there lay "the recognition of the main principle to advance which we are beginning our agitation"—*i.e.*, that a dealing with the labour question by legislative means is essential. Further, Lassalle declares, "the promise of the King that this dealing with the labour question, and the doing away with the misery of the workers, shall be brought about by legislative means;" and, thirdly, as "a Progressist Chamber, a Chamber elected by the Three-Class Electoral Law, would never vote the money necessary to the King for this object, or even, could this object be attained without money, would ever give their consent to such legislation;" the kingly promise, "through the intrinsic force of logic, included also a promise of universal and direct suffrage."

At these words the report represents "the meeting which had listened to the whole of this last part of the speech with extraordinary keenness," as "bursting into indescribable cheers," starting afresh every time Lassalle tried to continue his speech.

---

[1] The passage reads thus : "With the hope of a very speedy legal settlement of the question, and thus of the redressing of their grievances, His Majesty dismissed the deputation. The royal promise will echo encouragingly and helpfully through all the valleys of the Riesengebirg, and will inspire many hundreds of honest, patient families with new hope and new strength for brave endurance."

If the cheers were really so loud, it proves that the workers took Lassalle's interpretation of the King's promises for current coin—the very worst evidence that could be given against this speech.

There can be no doubt that this speech was intended, so far as the workers were concerned, to urge them to the greatest and most enthusiastic activity on behalf of the Association, by painting the success already achieved in the most brilliant colours possible. But the speech was intended for others besides working-men. In reply to a review of his "Bastiat-Schulze," published in the *Kreuz Zeitung*, and emanating, according to Lassalle, "from too important a source" for him to ignore the questions there addressed to him, he especially refers the reviewer in the Government organ to the Ronsdorf speech, and sends his reply and two copies of the speech under cover "personally" to Bismarck. Both speech and review were intended to make an impression upon the *Government*—were written *ad usum delphini.* The "indescribable cheers" were to be a bait for Bismarck and the King.

But no one man can serve two masters. The attempt to turn the speech so that it should produce the desired effect in higher quarters really gave it an out-and-out Cæsarian character. It is doubly a pronunciamento of Cæsarism—Cæsarism within the ranks of the party, and Cæsarism in the politics of the party.

" Yes, there is nothing more incapable of organisation and more impotent, nothing more unintelligent," writes Lassalle in his reply to the *Kreuz Zeitung*, "than the restless, malcontent, liberal individualism, this great malady of our time ! But this restless, malcontent individualism is by no means a malady of the masses ; it is, indeed, necessarily and naturally rooted only in the fractional intelligences of the bourgeoisie."

" The reason is obvious : the spirit of the masses, as behoves their position as masses, is always directed towards objective, positive aims. The voices of restless, vain-glorious individuals would be drowned in this volume of voices without even being heard. The oligarchical is the only homogeneous fruitful soil for the negative, acrid individualism of our Liberal bourgeoisie, and its subjective, obstinate self-glorification." And so, in the Ronsdorf speech, he says :

" There is another, a most remarkable element in our success, upon which I must touch. That is the solid spirit of complete *unity and discipline* that prevails in our Association ! And in this respect, too, in this respect above all, perhaps, our Association stands out—epoch-making, an entirely new figure in history ! This great Association, spreading over well-nigh all German lands, moves and has its being with the solid unity of an individual ! I am personally known to, and have personally visited but a small number of districts, and yet from the Rhine to the North Sea, and from the Elbe to the Danube, I have never heard a '*No ;*' and, at the same time, the authority with which you have invested me is one that rests entirely upon your own continued confidence in me ! . . . Wherever I have been, I have heard words from the workers, that may be summed up in the sentence : We must weld the wills of all of us into one single hammer, and must place this hammer in the hands of a man in whose intelligence, integrity, and good faith we have the necessary confidence, so that he may be able with that hammer to strike !

" The two contradictories which our statesmen have heretofore regarded as irreconcilable, whose fusion they have looked upon as the philosopher's stone—freedom and authority—these most extreme contradictories have been completely reconciled by our Association, which thus becomes on a small scale the prototype of our next form of society on a large scale. With us there is not a trace of that malcontent spirit of Liberalism, of that malady of individual opinion and superiority with which the body of our bourgeoisie is eaten up. . . ." [1]

There is a formally correct idea underlying these words, *i.e.*,

[1] " Die Agitation des Allgemeinen Deutschen Arbeitervereins," etc. (" The Agitation of the General German Working-men's Association,") 1st Edition, p. 37, etc.

that in modern Society the workers are under normal conditions
compelled to common action far more than any other class of
society ; and that, in fact, the very conditions of life of the modern
industrial proletarian, develop in him the spirit of solidarity. The
bourgeois, on the contrary, is only impelled towards common
action by abnormal conditions, and not by the very nature of his
social existence. This correct idea, however, receives a totally
false interpretation by the above generalisation. The action of
the masses does not, by a long way, mean personal dictatorship :
indeed, where the masses abdicate their will, they are already
on the road to become, from a revolutionary factor, a reactionary one. In the struggles of modern Society, personal
dictatorship has invariably been the sheet-anchor of the reactionary
classes, seeing their existence imperilled ; no one is so ready to
renounce " negative acrid individualism " as the modern bourgeois
so soon as his money bags and his class privileges seem seriously
threatened. In such moments the cry of " a reactionary mass "
becomes a true one, and when the tendency becomes a general
one Bonapartism flourishes. The classes that feel themselves incapable of self-government do that which Lassalle is here imputing
to the workers : they abdicate their own will in favour of a single
person, and condemn every attempt to oppose any private interests
of this person as " restless, malcontent individualism." Thus, in
the seventies and eighties, the German bourgeoisie accused the
very party—the Freisinnige—which was most consistently defending their class interests, of betraying these interests, because
by their " malcontent " they were hampering the self-preserving
activity of the State. And so in 1851, the French bourgeoisie
attacked their own parliamentary representatives, whenever they
attempted to refuse Louis Bonaparte the means for his *coup d'état*,
as "disturbers of the peace," "anarchists," etc., until Napoleon
was strong enough to proclaim himself dictator *against* the
bourgeoisie, instead of contenting himself with the *rôle* of mere
maintainer of law and order *for* the bourgeoisie.

A growing revolutionary class has absolutely no reason to
abdicate its will, to renounce the right of criticism, to renounce

its "superiority," vis-a-vis of its leaders. And we have seen, in the Solingen affair, that whatever stress Lassalle might lay upon his superior intelligence, vis-a-vis of the workers, it was from amongst the ranks of these workers that he had had to take a very distinct and energetic "No," and that surely not to the detriment of the movement. In Berlin, too, on one particular occasion, he had to take a like "No," and when he boasted at the Association directed by him that he had realised "authority and freedom" as represented above, he was expressing a wish rather than stating an actual fact.

In addition to those personal qualities of Lassalle's which made the idea of such dictatorship so sympathetic to him, there was now too actual need for it. The policy he was pursuing could only be carried through if the members and adherents of the movement followed their leader without criticism, and did his bidding without a murmur. Just as Lassalle himself dealt with the promise of the King of Prussia to the Silesian weavers in such a fashion that only by a small, quite casual reservation, did the democrat,—one is tempted to say—salve his conscience—while the rest meant nothing but pure Cæsarism; so his adherents also were to be ready, on the word of command, to don the livery of loyalty. If there is one thing that can at least humanly excuse the Ronsdorf speech, it is the fact that it was, under the given circumstances, a necessity for Lassalle. He needed the dictatorship in order to be sure of the workers whenever he should require them for his actual ends, and he needed the endorsement of his dictatorship to appear to those in higher circles as a power to be treated with. The speech was the necessary step in the path once entered upon—it was no longer possible to stop.

And so the subsequent steps taken by Lassalle, both as regards the internal management of the Association, and its immediate external action, followed in the same direction. In the Association he insisted upon the expulsion of Vahlteich, who had opposed him in matters concerning organisation. And he not only made this a Cabinet question—he or I?—so that the members of the Association had hardly any other choice than to sacrifice the working-man

Vahlteich to the president, he also acted most unloyally in this affair in other ways. Thus, *e.g.*, he gave directions for having the very voluminous written indictment he had drawn up against Vahlteich circulated in such a way that Vahlteich himself only learned its contents after it had already influenced the rest of the members of the executive against him.

Now, whatever one may think of Vahlteich s proposals for changes in the organisation, the way in which Lassalle represented the mere idea of a reform of the Association as treachery, was the less justified that he, Lassalle himself, had already half made up his mind to drop the Association if his last attempt "to bring pressure to bear upon events" should fail.

This attempt, or, as Lassalle himself has called it, this "coup," was to be carried out at Hamburg. It had reference to the affairs of the Duchies of Schleswig-Holstein, just then conquered from Denmark.

When, in the winter of 1863, the death of the King of Denmark forced the Schleswig-Holstein question to the front, Lassalle, who was at this time already in communication with Bismarck, and therefore had every interest to induce the Association to support any policy upon which the Prussian Government should decide, had been working up the members of the Association against the "Schleswig-Holstein craze," [1] and had drawn up and had everywhere got a resolution passed in which it was said that :

"The unification of Germany would of itself settle the Schleswig-Holstein question. In the face of this *great mission*, the question—so long as there are thirty-three princes in Germany—whether one of these is a foreign prince seems of comparatively very subordinate interest."

---

[1] In a letter of Lassalle's to the vice-president, Dr. Dammer—to whom Lassalle in the first excitement sent two absolutely contradictory telegrams —he actually said : "The first telegram I sent off at once because the whole Schleswig-Holstein craze is, in many respects, extremely unpleasant for me." The contradiction in the telegrams is now explained by the position, full of contradictions, into which Lassalle had drifted. He was, without knowing it himself, no longer free.

For the rest, the resolution is made up only of more or less general phrases. It was the duty of all German Governments to enforce, " if need be by force of arms," the incorporation of the Duchies with Germany, but the people are warned to be on their guard ; " to let themselves be drawn away from their great central mission by nothing." Against the Progressists and members of the *National Verein* the reproach is levelled of " seeming to want to use Schleswig-Holstein as an opportunity for diverting attention from the internal situation, and for shirking the solution of a conflict to which they are not equal, under the guise of Patriotism." This in the December of 1863.

The Duchies were now conquered, and the question was what to do with them. A large proportion of the Progressists were in favour of the legitimate claims of the Duke of Augustenburg, whilst the influential Prussian circles were for the annexation of the Duchies to Prussia. Now, however little interest the Democratic Parties had in adding a thirty-fourth to the already existing thirty-three sovereign princes in Germany, they, on the other hand, had no reason for conferring any augmentation of power upon the most reactionary Government in Germany at that time. Lassalle, however, had now so completely lost all his sense of political tact, that he in all seriousness contemplated holding a large public meeting at Hamburg, and getting it to pass a resolution to the effect that it was the *duty* of Bismarck to annex the Duchies to Prussia against the wishes of Austria and the other German States. No words are needed to point out what a part Lassalle thus took upon himself, nor for what a part he wanted to use the socialistically-inclined workers of Hamburg, who felt such warm gratitude and veneration for him. The project, however, was never carried out, and the Hamburg workers were happily spared a conflict between their democratic convictions, and their supposed duty towards their leader.

Lassalle, after fighting another lawsuit in Düsseldorf, had gone to Switzerland. His first stay was at Rigi Kaltbad, and here, on the occasion of an excursion, he received an invitation from Fräulein Helene von Dönniges, whose acquaintance he had made in Berlin in the winter of 1861 to 1862, and to whom, according to her statements, he had already then offered his hand. Out of this visit grew that love affair whose final result was the premature death of Lassalle.

The details of the Lassalle-Dönniges affair are to-day so well known, all the steps taken by Lassalle in this business that are really characteristic of him are placed so absolutely beyond doubt, that a repetition of the whole story is unnecessary here. Moreover, during the affair Lassalle did not show himself in any new light;—he rather developed only such qualities as are already familiar to us;—it may, indeed, be said that the Dönniges affair on a small scale, and in another domain, is essentially a reproduction of the history of the Lassallean agitation. Lassalle believed he had found the wife of his choice in Helene von Dönniges. The only difficulty was to obtain the consent of the parents. But Lassalle had not the faintest doubt that the influence of his personality must overcome this difficulty. Self-consciously, and yet at the same time with circumspect calculation of every possible contingency, he drew up his plan of campaign. He will come, will conquer the good-will of the parents, and wring from them their consent before they really know what they are doing in acquiescing. Then suddenly a small unforeseen obstacle comes in the way. Through the indiscretion of the young lady the parents learn earlier than they should do of the engagement, and declare that they will not accept Lassalle as son-in-law under any circumstances. Lassalle, however, does not yet give up his plan. His triumph will only be greater the greater the opposition of the parents. Strong in his self-confidence, he takes a step which gives such a turn to the situation, that all hope of attaining his end in the way planned out is excluded, a step that shakes even the girl's own faith in him. . . . Well, then, if not in this way, then in another. And regardless of what he owes himself and his political position, Lassalle begins a struggle in which there is for him but one point of view—success. Every means is right that promises success. Spies are employed to watch the Dönniges family, and to report

their every movement. Through the instrumentality of Hans
von Bülow, Richard Wagner is entreated to induce the King of
Bavaria to intervene on Lassalle's behalf with Herr von Dönniges,
while Bishop Ketteler, of Mainz, is offered Lassalle's conversion
to Catholicism, in order that the Bishop may exercise his influence
in Lassalle's favour. Lassalle did not in the least care how unworthy it was of the historical mission he had set himself, to
dance attendance upon a Minister von Schrenck, so that the latter
might help him to his love, nor did he care how little worthy
he was proving himself of his prototype Hutten, when he
petitioned the incarnate representative of Rome to help him to
obtain a wife. Here where he might have shown pride, where he
should have shown it, he did not.

And yet success did not come. The Bishop of Mainz could
do nothing, because Helene von Dönniges was a Protestant, and
the attempted mediation undertaken by confidential representatives sent to the scene of the struggle by the Bavarian Minister
for Foreign Affairs only seemed to prove to Lassalle that by his
method of proceeding he had placed himself and the woman he
was fighting for in a totally false position.

Although he knew that Helene was absolutely without
strength of will, and had indeed perceived in this an advantage
for his future life together with her—"Keep Helene for me in the
submissive frame of mind in which she now is," he had written on
the 2nd August to the Countess Hatzfeld—he all at once expected her to do that which demanded a very strong will, and
was indignant because she tried to back out of it. Upheld by
his self-esteem, and accustomed to look at things exclusively from
the point of view of his own moods and interests, he had entirely
left out of his calculations that it is the most submissive
human beings who most easily change their impressions, and thus
he saw "boundless treachery," and the "most-unheard-of trick"
of an "abandoned jade," where there was nothing more than the
instability of a grisette in high life.

Meantime, however, his nervous system was completely shattered, and for a long while he no longer possessed the energy

of a healthy will. Sudden resort to violent means, anxiety to move heaven and earth about every petty matter, inability to bear with contradiction, or to deny oneself any desire, are not proofs of mental strength, but of extreme weakness. And the rapid alternations between outbursts of anger and of tears that, according to the unanimous testimony of eye-witnesses, at this time manifested themselves in Lassalle, point unmistakably to an absolutely shattered nervous system.

In this condition it was impossible for him to take his defeat quietly, and he sought to obtain satisfaction in a duel for the insult which, in his opinion, had been offered him. Foolish as duelling is in itself, it was comprehensible enough under these circumstances. In the circles of society in which this affair occurred, a duel is the cleansing bath that removes all stain and all insult, and if Lassalle had not the moral strength to resort— no matter what he was fighting for—only to means such as became the representative of the party of the socialistic reorganisation of Society, then it was but logical that he should try to obtain satisfaction for the supposed insult offered after the fashion of his surroundings.

He who faced the Bojard Janko von Racowitza in duel was not the Socialist Lassalle, but Lassalle the would-be aristocrat merchant's son, and if in the person of the latter the former, *i.e.*, the Socialist, was also shot down in the duel, he thereby expiated the sin of having allowed his other self to gain the ascendancy.

CHAPTER X.

THUS did an early death abruptly end Lassalle's political career, his plans and hopes. Perhaps it was well so, perhaps in his last hours he himself did not think it a misfortune. The goal that he had believed he could take by storm had again receded into the distance, and for the quiet work of organisation he 'id not believe himself fitted. Thus his immediate future seemeᴅ ᴠroblematical enough, and this may have contributed largely to ᴛhe almost frantic passion with which he threw himself into the Dönniges affair.

No doubt it is idle to speculate as to what Lassalle might have done if he had not fallen beneath the bullet of Herr von Racowitza. And yet this question has hitherto been, for the most part, answered in such a way as to justify a brief examination of it.

For it is generally contended, that had Lassalle lived, there would have been nothing left for him, as things were, but to follow the example of his friend Bucher, and to accept office in the service of the Prussian State. But this is to judge Lassalle quite wrongly. Certainly, the policy finally adopted by him must, if logically carried out, have led him at last into the Government camp, but it is just this last step which Lassalle would not himself have taken. He would never have donned the Prussian livery. He possessed sufficient means to live as he pleased, and such a post as the Prussian Government could offer him, would have no more satisfied his ambition, than it would have been congenial to his innermost and always unchanged convictions. In this respect he could rather have said to Bismarck than Bismarck to him : " What canst thou, poor devil, give "

185

It is far more probable that as soon as the sentences pronounced against him had come into effect, he would have permanently settled down abroad, and there awaited some change in the conditions of things in Prussia and in Germany. For it is self-evident that the Hamburg "coup," even though the meeting had been held, and the resolution passed, would have had practically no effect upon the actual situation. How poor the outlook was may be seen from the fact that the mere consent of Helene von Dönniges had sufficed to seriously shake Lassalle's opinion as to the probable effect of the "coup." On the 27th July, he had written of this project to the Countess Hatzfeld : "I must get to Hamburg first, where I am going to make a *great, very great,* perhaps *really* IM-PORTANT 'coup'." The following day he obtains Helene's consent to be his wife, and then writes to the Countess that he doesn't promise himself "anything much" from the Hamburg attempt. The passage referred to in this letter has certainly been quoted very often, but as it is extremely characteristic of Lassalle's mood at this time, it may again be quoted here. It runs :

"How you misunderstand me when you write : 'Cannot you, for a time, be satisfied with science, friendship, and the beauties of nature?' You think I must have politics.

"Ah! how little you are *au fait* with me. *I desire nothing more ardently than to be quite rid of all politics,* in order to devote myself to science, friendship, and nature. I am *sick and tired* of politics. Truly, I would burn as passionately for them as ever if there were *anything serious to be done,* or if I had the *power,* or saw the means to bring it about—such means as should benefit me—FOR WITHOUT SUPREME POWER NOTHING CAN BE DONE. *For child's play, however, I am too old and too great.* That is why I very reluctantly undertook the presidentship! I only yielded to *you.* And that is why it now weighs upon me terribly. If I were but rid of it, *this* were the moment when I should decide to go to Naples with you! But how get rid of it?

"For events, I fear, will develop slowly, slowly, and my glowing soul finds no joy in these children's maladies, and chronic processes. Politics mean *actual, immediate* activity. Everything else can be

done as well by science. I shall try to exercise PRESSURE on events
in Hamburg. What the effect will be, I cannot say, nor do I
promise myself anything much from it !

"Ah ! could I but get out of it ! "

In another passage in the same letter, Lassalle writes that he is
" in good spirits and full of strength," and, "well, the old strength
is still there, and the old good luck too." They were, therefore,
essentially political considerations which dictated these lines full
of resignation.

When, after his stay with Helene von Dönniges at Bern, Lassalle arrived on the 3rd August at Geneva, he appears to have
made up his mind as to provisional expatriation. Among the
papers of Johann Philipp Becker, there is a *permis de séjour* of the
Geneva Government made out for " M. Ferdinand Lassalle, *pro-
fesseur*," living " Chez M. Becker," and upon the wrapper the following remarks in the hand of the old veteran of freedom :

" When friend Lassalle, on his arrival in the fatal year 1864,
told me that he felt his strength exhausted, and that he must give
himself pause ; that he had believed he could bring the Socialist
movement to a head in about one year, but that he now saw that
it would take decades, for which he did not feel his physical
strength sufficient, and that, above all, he could never stand the impending imprisonment ; hereupon I advised him under these
circumstances, to seek a definite residence somewhere, and to this
end, at once to settle down in Geneva, and when in conformity
with the law, he could prove a two years' sojourn, to have himself
naturalised, which would have caused no difficulty at this time.
Meanwhile, he could, of course, travel as much as he liked.
Lassalle unhesitatingly agreed, and on the 11th August, 1864, I
obtained for him the *permis de séjour*."

The permit itself is made out for six months.

During the four weeks of his struggle for Helene von Dönniges,
the letters that reached Lassalle from the Secretariat of the
General German Working-men's Association, were not even an-

swered by him. It was only on the evening before the duel, when
making his will, that he again remembered the Association, and
left its Secretary, Willms, 500 thalers a year for five years, for
purposes of agitation, and 150 thalers a year for his personal use.
He recommended the Frankfort delegate, Bernhard Becker, as his
own successor. He was to hold fast to the organisation ; " it will
lead the working-class to victory."

Among the members of the Association, the news of Lassalle's
death caused no little consternation. For a long time it was impossible for them to grasp the idea that Lassalle had actually
fallen in a mere ordinary love affair. They believed in a pre-
meditated plot hatched by his opponents to get rid of the
dangerous agitator, and did homage to the fallen man as the
victim of a vile political intrigue. A veritable Lassalle cult now
grew up, a kind of Lassalle religion, the propagation of which was,
above all, stimulated—for very natural reasons—by the Countess
Hatzfeld. The personal attitude which Lassalle had adopted to
the workers also contributed largely to this cult. Amiable as he
could be in his intercourse with them, he had constantly taken
care to impress upon them both by his outward appearance
and his manners, his social and mental superiority. Further, he
had with the utmost complacency allowed himself to be fêted at
Ronsdorf as a kind of founder of a new religion, and had himself
taken care that an account exaggerating the actual occurrences
should appear in the *Nordstern*.

In his speeches his own personality had come more and more
to the front—to such an extent that when he spoke of himself in
connection with others, he had invariably put the I first.

Some persons may have been repelled by this attitude, but upon
the masses, especially in the salad days of the movement, it cast a
great charm, and the more a legendary halo invested the personality of Lassalle, the greater became the after-effects of that
charm.

It would, however, be altogether a mistake to deny the fact that
this cult for the personality of Lassalle did, for a long time, greatly
help on the movement. When all is said and done most persons

like to see a cause, which, the more far-reaching its aims at any given moment, must seem the more abstract, embodied in one individual. This craving to personify a cause is the secret of the success of most founders of religions, whether charlatans or visionaries, and in England and America it is a recognised factor in political party-struggles. This craving is so strong, that at times the bare fact that a certain personality has withdrawn himself from a body of men, his equals or even his superiors, is sufficient to raise him above them, and to procure him a power that has been obstinately refused them. We have only to recall the Boulanger fever in France, which is by no means without its prototypes in the history of other countries. Dozens of members of the French Chamber were Boulanger's superiors in knowledge, ability, and character, and could point to the most honourable scars gained in the service of the Republic, but they became mere ciphers side by side with him, whilst he became the great One, and his name enkindled hundreds of thousands. Why? Because an idea was suddenly incorporated in him, while the Chamber of Deputies, despite the sum of knowledge and of experience which it represented, was nothing but an anonymous quantity.

The name Lassalle became a standard which created more and more enthusiasm among the masses the more Lassalle's works spread among the people. Intended to produce immediate effect, written with extraordinary talent, popular, and yet setting forth the theoretical points of view, they had, and to a certain extent still have to-day, a great effect in agitation. "The Working-men's Programme," the "Open Reply Letter," the "Worker's Reader," etc., have won over hundreds of thousands to Socialism. The strength of conviction that breathes in these writings has enkindled hundreds of thousands to struggle for the rights of labour. And with this, Lassalle's writings never degenerate into a jingle of meaningless phrases : they are pervaded by a sensible realism, which certainly at times is mistaken as to means, but always seeks to keep actual facts in sight, qualities which have through his writings been communicated to the movement. That whereof Lassalle in practice had, perhaps, something too much, he has given, in his first and

best propagandist works, the right measure which the working-class
movement required.   If the German Social Democracy has always
recognised the value of a strong organisation, if it has been so convinced of the necessity of the concentration of forces, that even
without the outer bond of organisation it has yet known how to
perform all the functions of one, this is largely a heritage of the
agitation of Lassalle. It is an indisputable fact that in those
places where, amongst the workers, the traditions of the Lassallean
agitation were strongest, as a rule, most was accomplished in the
way of organisation.

However, one cannot have the advantages of a thing without
having to accept its disadvantages into the bargain.   We have
seen what a doubly two-edged weapon the Lassallean agitation
was, two-edged in its theoretical foundation, two-edged in its
practice.   And this continued, of course, long after Lassalle himself was dead.   Aye, it became worse.   Adhesion to Lassalle's
tactics meant adhesion to the change of front executed by Lassalle
during the last months of his agitation, he himself knowing, and
making the mental reservation that he should be able to turn
back and throw off the mask at any moment.   But in his own
words : " individuals can dissemble, the masses never." His policy,
if literally carried out, meant misleading the masses.   And the
masses were misled.   The time of the Schweitzer dictatorship
came.   Whether Herr von Schweitzer was ever, in the literal
sense of the word, a Government agent, seems to me very doubtful ; but there can be no doubt that his tactics were at times
those of a Government agent.   Why, under his leadership, it
even came to this, that agitators of the " General German Working-men's Association" declared a republican to be synonymous
with a bourgeois, because republics so far have been bourgeois
republics.   Schweitzer was unquestionably the most gifted of
Lassalle's successors.   But if he almost equalled Lassalle in
talent, he surpassed him in all his worst faults.   He was a real
cynic, and he therefore coquetted with the Social demagogues of
the Prussian Court with even less hesitation than Lassalle had done.
But that he should have been able to do this without once failing

to find some passage justifying his manœuvres in Lassalle's speeches is a reproach from which Lassalle cannot escape. Even Schweitzer has done nothing worse than to designate as a simple "clique" the parties that were fighting for the constitutional rights of the people's representatives, among whom were men like Jacoby, Waldeck, Ziegler, etc.

Other faults of Lassalle's also were reproduced in the movement, and it cost long and sharp struggles before they were completely overcome. As to the theoretical errors of Lassalle, which I have dealt with more fully above, I need here only remind my readers what violent struggles it cost before a right appreciation of the Trades Union movement could make headway in the ranks of the German Socialist working-men ; how long Trades Unions were opposed by a large portion of the Socialists, on the strength of the "iron law of wages." The result of the personal colour that Lassalle gave the movement, was that after his death it drifted into the current of sectarianism, and floundered about in it for long years to come.

Persons who have played a prominent part, and developed remarkable qualities, usually beget a large number of imitators. So, too, Lassalle. The semi and semi-demi Lassalles after his death blossomed forth all over the land. But since for want of his ability, they were forced to confine themselves to imitating, "Wie er sich geräuspert, und wie er gespuckt,"[1] and as we have seen, this not being his best side, they formed one of the most obnoxious excrescences of the working-class movement.

To-day all this has been overcome, and we can speak of it quietly, and without bitterness. But there was a time when the movement suffered from it, and that is why it is referred to here.

But enough. Else the impression of what I have said of the heritage which Lassalle left the workers, even to this day, might be weakened, and this is by no means my intention. So long as I had to consider Lassalle's work in detail, I was bound to be severe ; for greater than the fame of the individual is the interest of the great cause for which we are fighting, and that above all

[1] "The way he hawked, and the way he spat."

else demands the truth. The Social Democracy has no legends, and needs none; it regards its champions not as saints but as men. It does not, on this account, value their services the less, but honours the memory of those who have done well in the work of freeing the working-class.

And this Lassalle did in an eminent degree. Perhaps in a more eminent degree than he himself suspected on the eve of his death. Things came about differently from what he believed they would; but the movement to-day is the same as that for which he raised the standard in the spring of 1863. The ends for which it strives are the same to-day, even though they be striven for in other ways and with other demands. A few years hence it may, perhaps, be fighting in yet other ways, and still it will be the same movement.

No man, even the greatest thinker, can foretell the march of Social Democracy in detail. We know not how many struggles still lie before us, nor how many fighters will have to perish before the goal of the movement is reached; but the grave-stones of our dead tell us of the progress of the movement, and fill us with the certainty of its triumph in the future.

Lassalle no more created German Social Democracy than any other man. We have seen how great were the stir and ferment among the advanced German workers, when Lassalle placed himself at the head of the movement. But even though he cannot be called the creator of the movement, yet to Lassalle belongs the honour of having done great things for it, greater than falls to the lot of most single individuals to achieve. Where at most there was only a vague desire, he gave conscious effort; he trained the German workers to understand their historical mission, he taught them to organise as an independent political party, and in this way at least accelerated by many years the process of development of the movement. His actual undertaking failed, but his struggle for it was not in vain; despite failure, it brought the working-class nearer to the goal. The time for victory was not yet, but in order to conquer, the workers must first learn to fight. And to have trained them for the fight, to have, as the song says, given them swords, this remains the great, the undying merit of Ferdinand Lassalle.

THE END.